As I Have Loved You

AS I HAVE LOVED YOU

CLERICAL UNITY IN THE HEART OF CHRIST

Deacon Dominic Cerrato, PhD

Our Sunday Visitor
Huntington, Indiana

Nihil Obstat
Msgr. Michael Heintz, Ph.D.
Censor Librorum

Imprimatur
✠ Kevin C. Rhoades
Bishop of Fort Wayne-South Bend
January 12, 2025

Scripture texts in this work are taken from the *Revised Standard Version of the Bible*—Second Catholic Edition (Ignatius Edition) Copyright © 2006 National Council of the Churches of Christ in the United States of America. Used by permission. All rights reserved worldwide.

Excerpts from the English translation of the *Catechism of the Catholic Church* for use in the United States of America Copyright © 1994, United States Catholic Conference, Inc.—Libreria Editrice Vaticana. Used with Permission. English translation of the *Catechism of the Catholic Church*: Modifications from the *Editio Typica* copyright © 1997, United States Conference of Catholic Bishops—Libreria Editrice Vaticana.

Every reasonable effort has been made to determine copyright holders of excerpted materials and to secure permissions as needed. If any copyrighted materials have been inadvertently used in this work without proper credit being given in one form or another, please notify Our Sunday Visitor in writing so that future printings of this work may be corrected accordingly.

Our Sunday Visitor Publishing Division
Our Sunday Visitor, Inc.
200 Noll Plaza
Huntington, IN 46750
www.osv.com
1-800-348-2440

ISBN: 978-1-63966-300-2 (Inventory No. T2955)
1. RELIGION—Clergy.
2. RELIGION—Christianity—Catholic.

eISBN: 978-1-63966-301-9
LCCN: 2025931974

Cover and interior design: Amanda Falk
Cover and interior art: *Last Supper* by Peter Paul Rubens/Restored Traditions

PRINTED IN THE UNITED STATES OF AMERICA

CONTENTS

FOREWORDS

It's quite unusual for a book to have more than one foreword. However, because this work aims at three distinct but related readers — bishops, priests, and deacons — it has three corresponding forewords, each speaking not simply to their own office but, in and through their particular office, to all grades of those who share in holy orders.

From the Perspective of a Bishop

What a blessing that my entire ordained life has been lived out in two of the dioceses in the world that have a very large quantity of deacons serving within them — namely, the Archdiocese of Chicago and the Diocese of Joliet, in Illinois. For me, this reality has always been a gift and source of great happiness. I was ordained a deacon, a priest, and a bishop all in the Archdiocese of Chicago. In 2020, I was installed as the sixth Bishop of Joliet. In this context, I met Deacon Dominic Cerrato. After three years of serving and working with him, my respect for him continues to grow. He loves God with all his mind, heart, and soul, and has a true call to live and promote the call to service (*diakonia*) in the Church. His gentle and warm personality is complemented by his keen intellect with a strong desire to teach and form others. Not only does he share his gifts as the director of the Office of the Diaconate in the Diocese of Joliet, but he also serves nationally as the editor for Our Sunday Visitor's *The Deacon* magazine and as a member of the international Papal Commission on Women and the Diaconate.

When I first glanced at the title of Deacon Dominic's book, I immediately wondered if some people might take issue with the word *clerical*. Today, in the context of our modern Church, that word is often peppered with some negative connotations. Or more accurately, it is conflated with the word *clericalism*.

Clericalism points to an abuse of power, status, or privilege mixed in with a sense of superiority both individually and institutionally. Whereas, being ordained for the "clerical" state is rooted in a true call from Christ to serve with humility and love, and a desire for the common good. Historically, "clericalism" has produced many negative consequences for our Church. Indeed, we are still paying the price for some of them.

However, Deacon Dominic masterfully distinguishes and explains the differences between the words *cleric* and *clericalism*. Throughout this book, when referring to the offices of bishops, priests, and deacons, he unequivocally refutes and rejects any desire for "clericalism." Simultaneously, he gives a healthy, practical, and holy perspective as to what true clerical unity could and should look like.

One of the many ways he does this is by addressing the need for proper identity of bishops, priests, and deacons in order to promote unity within the mission and their respective ministries. This resonates with a portion of my operative theology, which focuses on everyone's identity being formed in the image and likeness of God. We are beloved sons and daughters of God the Father, whose love for us is unconditional. Deacon Dominic builds on this foundation and presents the ways in which solid and strong formation is needed not only to form and shape the identity of deacons, but also to shape how deacons, priests, and bishops all relate to each other.

Although Deacon Dominic's thoughts and ideas contained in this book are certainly scholarly and thought-provoking, I also want to highlight how he rightly insists that if true clerical unity is to flourish, then there must be a practical path forward. As someone who is goal-oriented and likes to produce real change for the better both for individuals and systems, I am personally delighted that Deacon Dominic clearly spells out the process to accomplish this. He also encourages the reader to develop and follow a concrete plan with his useful steps and stages.

Each day, I continue to thank God for this call to ordained ministry and service in the Catholic Church. This gratitude overflows with the opportunity to know and work in the vineyard with so many talented and holy bishops, priests, and deacons who share in the order of the diaconate. Ultimately, we are united through, with, and in Christ. May that unity continue to grow and be realized as we follow this beautiful and practical roadmap provided by Deacon Dominic Cerrato.

Most Reverend Ronald Aldon Hicks
Diocese of Joliet

From the Perspective of a Priest

"The Lord appointed seventy others, and sent them on ahead of him, two by two, into every town and place where he himself was about to come" (Lk 10:1). Since the days of the early Church, this communal pattern of ministry, set by the Lord Jesus himself, has offered a paradigmatic blueprint for those who would undertake the mission of evangelization. St. Gregory the Great says of this passage, "The Lord sends his disciples out to preach in twos in order to teach us silently that whoever fails in charity toward his neighbor should by no means take upon himself the office of preaching." From the start, and by divine design, ministry was never meant to be a solo endeavor. Indeed, radical individualism is one of the most destructive counter-witnesses to the spread of the Gospel.

This book by Deacon Dominic Cerrato offers a further contribution to the perennial theme of unity in ministry by emphasizing that the three grades of holy orders are meant, by Jesus' own design, to work together as one. Rather than basing the idea of clerical unity on pragmatic, utilitarian, or functional grounds, Deacon Dominic roots the unity of the clergy in the fact that the Sacrament of Holy Orders has been established by the Lord as *one* sacrament. If it is indeed a single sacrament in three grades, then each grade must understand that the brotherhood of holy orders is not simply a brotherhood either between bishops, or between priests, or between deacons, but far more organically, a brotherhood which unites the three grades as one. This beautiful truth must be understood, cultivated, and lived out in ministry if the ordained are to be faithful to the design that the Lord Jesus himself established from the start.

Inevitably, many factors get in the way. The historical ebb and flow of the diaconate over the centuries; patterns of parish organization and politics; an overly functional approach to ministry; all of these conspire to obscure the essential unity of the three grades of orders with deleterious effects for the Church. With this book, Deacon Dominic seeks to offer new insights and thus fresh energy to ordained ministry by reminding bishops, priests, and deacons of the one call given to all three grades to embody Christ the Servant sacramentally in their lives.

The theme of unity is ever more critical. Fragmentation and tribalism are tragic hallmarks of our modern culture, which atomizes individuals and groups into ever smaller camps. The

Church is not immune to these trends. Even the shortest exposure to Catholic social media can lead one to despair that the Church is just a religious subgroup embodying the same polarized and politicized dynamics that engulf society as a whole. To be a credible sign of the presence of Jesus in our world, to have any hope of effective evangelization, the Church and her ministers must rise above this, as Our Lord prayed, "that they may all be one; even as you, Father, are in me, and I in you, that they also may be in us, so that the world may believe that you have sent me" (Jn 17:21).

As the pastor of the parish in which Deacon Dominic ministers, I have been blessed to benefit experientially from this clerical unity between the grades of orders in a most fruitful way. Having spent some years of my priesthood in a parish without the ministry of deacons, it became clear to me that something was missing. Certainly, being a lone priest without any deacons (or other priests) is a heavier burden in terms of the workload of ministry, but there is more to it than that. As Deacon Dominic points out with his wonderful image of the triptych, this is far more than a functional issue. It is about more than just getting the work of ministry done. It is rather about showing forth the full image of the Church, the Bride of Christ, in all her beauty to the world. To paint this complete picture necessarily requires all three grades of holy orders.

I am grateful to Deacon Dominic for the ways in which he offers his "vision of an artist" to paint this picture of unified ordained ministry in my own parish and, with this book, for the wider Church. Our world needs to see the effective witness of what it means to live in unity, to work together as one in the vineyard, and to labor as brothers in helping to build the kingdom.

Fr. Gregory Rothfuchs, Pastor
St. Irene Catholic Church, Warrenville, Illinois

From the Perspective of a Deacon

Without a doubt, there is unity within holy orders as bishop, priest, and deacon constitute the one Christ, ministering to His Bride, the Church. Within holy orders, the one Christ extends His ministry in each epoch, and through the grades of holy orders, reveals something essential of His own mysterious identity and power. By way of the one Sacrament of Holy Orders, Christ teaches, governs, heals, forgives, unites, serves, and sends the members of His own Body into the world to proclaim the Good News.

What is in doubt is the existential and pastoral unity of the three grades as they express themselves in the lives of individual men. For over fifty years now, the Church has been attempting to form men called to the diaconate through "part-time" processes of formation. This type of formation is inevitable due to the inclusion in the diaconate of men called to the Sacrament of Marriage. This part-time formation has its limitations, one of the effects of which can be personal tensions between priests and deacons. As a result of the time limitations imposed upon diaconal formation, not all deacons achieve competency or maturation within the areas of personality development, liturgical assistance, preaching, teaching, and leadership skills. Priests tend to judge the achievement and execution of these realities by the standards they had to meet in seminary. This measure is unfair, but so is a formation process that may allow insufficiently formed men to be ordained deacons.

To address renewal in the relationships within holy orders, I would suggest a national review of the essentials of diaconal formation led by bishops and deacon formators. What aspects of the present practice of deacon formation are being overlooked or cursorily attended to and need to be made substantial during a diocese's in-person formation program, and what aspects may be achieved through online courses or in ongoing formation after ordination? We have lived with the diaconate long enough now to know that some aspects of formation clearly need more weight than others.

First, deacons need to become men of the Church, with Catholic imaginations. They need to learn how to pray and how to understand and love Scripture. They need to go deep into the sacramental and spiritual meaning of marriage, holy orders, and liturgy. They need endless hours of preaching practicums, a deep grasp of the social teachings of the Church, dynamic pastoral formation among the poor, sick, and spiritually hungry; and finally, they need an authentic development in the virtues of praying with and for other people. Attaining ministerial competency, spiritual conversion, and affective maturity will go a long way in helping priests see deacons as spiritual and ministerial collaborators on mission and not simply "help" that frees the priest for other ministerial priorities. When I was director of formation for an archdiocesan diaconate program, most requests from pastors to have deacons assigned to their parishes were to fulfill tasks any of the baptized could do. What they really needed were well-trained lay ministers, not brother clerics who could shoulder visioning and leadership duties alongside the pastor. Deacons should not simply be viewed as ordained "lay ministers." A new unified clerical imagination must be born.

This book can be a turning point in our understanding and practice of forming men in an authentic diaconal identity. I would hope it will become a source for common conversation among deacon formation directors and bishops on the topic of diaconal mission and formation for the next fifty years. For priests, this book, among others, should become incorporated into the curriculum and formation of diocesan seminaries. Clerics will never achieve working, cooperative unity and respect among themselves if seminarians continue to be formed as priests without substantial formation in the diaconate, an identity that remains dynamic within the priest for his life.

To have this book in the hands of all deacon leaders and, hopefully, in the hands of seminary formators can hasten the day when the Christological unity of holy orders is seen more clearly because our clerical unity has become more personal and concrete.

Deacon James Keating, Ph.D.
Kenrick-Glennon Seminary, St Louis, Missouri

Preface

In over forty years of pastoral ministry on both the parish and diocesan levels, I have seen and read much on the importance of the relationship between the clergy and the laity. The various documents and decrees following the Second Vatican Council acknowledged and promoted the laity, encouraging them to assume a more active role in the life and mission of the Church. This resulted in a number of lay ministries that spanned from liturgical to catechetical, from bringing Communion to the sick to engaging in the corporal works of mercy. This expansion, arising from a deeper appreciation of their baptismal call, began shortly after the council and grew slowly and steadily. Such growth required priests to "step back" from some traditional ministries to those more exclusive to their priesthood. Although most welcomed the change, others found it difficult.

As the laity were taking on greater ministerial responsibility through the 1970s, the expansion of the diaconate as a permanent order began to be felt. As more and more permanent deacons were ordained, especially in larger dioceses, many deacons experienced a kind of "pastoral squeeze" between priests who had already given ministerial ground to the laity and laity who didn't want to give up ministries to deacons, not realizing that laity could only exercise those particular ministries in the absence of a deacon. All of this, combined with a lack of catechetical formation on the nature and role of the diaconate in the life of the Church, resulted in a diaconal identity crisis. Quite often, permanent deacons were seen by the laity as affable old men who helped out around the parish — sort of "half-baked" priests who couldn't handle celibacy. Their vocation was viewed by some as a retirement ministry and, because young men with families were often actively discouraged from entering formation, the diaconate became kind of a "grandpa club."

A large part of the challenge is that deacons are often viewed as lay people who exercise special ministry, and not clerics who live a lay life. It's not popular today to be a cleric as, unfortunately, some identify being a cleric with clericalism. Where the former is a vocation from God, the latter is an abuse of that vocation. Within this context, *clericalism* refers to an excessive or unwarranted emphasis on the authority, privileges, or status of the clergy at the expense of the laity. It can manifest as an attitude, a set of behaviors, or a system of beliefs that separates the clergy from the laity and places the clergy in a superior or privileged position within the Church. Although this can exist between the clergy and the laity, it can also exist within and among the clergy. Clericalism has been rightly criticized for potentially fostering an environment that can enable abuses of power, hinder collaboration, and distance the clergy from themselves and the lived experiences of the faithful. At the 2023 Synod on Synodality in Rome, Pope Francis observed, "Clericalism is a scourge, it is a blow. It is a form of worldliness that defiles and damages the face of the Lord's bride; it enslaves the holy, faithful people of God."

Because deacons seek to fulfill their proper place in the

Church, a place often held by the laity in the deacon's absence, their ministry can, to the uninformed, appear as a form of clericalism. This is particularly true when exercising liturgical ministry, as when the deacon carries the Book of the Gospels or reads the Universal Prayer, or displaces an extraordinary minister of the Eucharist at Mass. Although this has diminished over the years, it's still quite prevalent in dioceses where deacons are few and far between. This false clericalism fails to understand that the diaconate is not about "power" as the world knows it but serving as Christ served, loving as Christ loved. As pointed out by Pope Francis in an address to the deacons of Rome:

> Let us remember, please, that for the disciples of Jesus, to love is to serve and to serve is to reign. Power lies in service, not in anything else. And as you have recalled what I say that deacons are the custodians of service in the Church, so we can say that they are the custodians of true "power" in the Church, so that no one goes beyond the power of service. Think about this.

For deacons to be accepted for who they are, for them to enter more fully into the Catholic imagination, they must assume with humility what they are: members of the clergy who live a lay life. This is to say deacons are called, by virtue of their ordination, to be clergy and exercise their *diakonia* within the whole of their life and ministry, whether as a husband or in the sanctuary, as a father or in ecclesial ministry; they are deacons at the core of their being. This is essential to clerical unity because unity requires, as a precondition, that each member of the community has a strong sense of self before he can give that same self to another. If there is an identity crisis among deacons, it will, as we shall see, impact the unity of all clergy. Moreover, inasmuch as all three degrees of holy orders ontologically share in the diaconate, a lack of recognition and appropriation of this order, even when it is exercised in the episcopate and presbyterate, will result in a tendency to seek to be served rather than serve.

This book is written for the clergy: for bishops, priests, deacons, seminarians, and men in diaconal formation. Its aim is to foster greater unity between and among the orders so as to more effectively fulfill the mission of the Church. Though written from the perspective of a deacon, I received considerable input from bishops and priests, as well as from other deacons. This perspective, of course, would be true of any member of the clergy, as we all write from a particular point of view. Although this perspective will be evident throughout this book, I suspect both bishops and priests will identify with much of what I write. Within this context, what follows are my own personal reflections as a deacon and private theologian. They carry no more weight than the compelling nature of my arguments or lack thereof. They are offered simply as a starting point for a much larger conversation and arise out of love of God and neighbor.

Ultimately, what follows in this book is an exercise of my own *diakonia*, imperfect though it is. It's offered in fraternal love to my fellow members of the clergy so that, together and in union with Christ, the Church's mission may be fulfilled in us and God be glorified.

INTRODUCTION

SOME PRELIMINARY CONSIDERATIONS

The Church of the future lies in the present. This observation may seem rather apparent, so much so that it can be easily dismissed. Indeed, all things move chronologically from the past into the present and from the present into the future. However, within this obvious reality lies a profound truth — namely, that what we do today has, to a greater or lesser extent, an impact on what happens tomorrow. Put another way, our concrete choices have a causal relationship with what follows. Understood this way, past, present, and future aren't three independent things, but three distinct parts of the same reality forming one sole organic path in which free will plays an essential, albeit limited role.

In making this observation, it's important to recognize that this causal relationship arising out of free will is not perfect. It's not as though we do this one thing and then that other intended thing necessarily happens. Although we have some influence over the future, life is far too unpredictable to always have the desired outcome. Other factors inside and outside of ourselves may intervene, diminishing the wanted effect or even eliminating it entirely. Still, within these limitations, there exists a profound freedom that, together with our intellect and governed by faith, enables us to influence change by virtue of the exercise of our will.

Bearing this in mind, we might ask a few important questions. What will the Church, notably on the parish level, look like ten, twenty, or even one hundred years from now? More to the point, what can we do as bishops, priests, and deacons to effect a change for the better and advance the mission with which we've been entrusted?

The Church of the Future

To begin grappling with this question, we would do well to consider the observations of a young Bavarian theologian, Fr. Joseph Ratzinger. In a 1969 broadcast on German radio, the future Pope Benedict XVI spoke prophetically of a future where the Church would be smaller. Bear in mind that, at the time he spoke, the Church was still in the honeymoon stage of the Second Vatican Council. Priestly and religious vocations were strong, and the pews were full. Nonetheless, the Church was already experiencing a kind of crisis of faith as witnessed by the release of *Humanae Vitae* and the public dissent by some theologians. Bubbling beneath the surface and fueled by moral relativism expressed in the sexual revolution, the Church was faced with a new threat. In the midst of this, Father Ratzinger wrote:

> From the crisis of today the Church of tomorrow will emerge — a Church that has lost much. She will become small and will have to start afresh more or less from the beginning. She will no longer be able to inhabit many of the edifices she built in prosperity. As the number

of her adherents diminishes, so it will lose many of her social privileges. … But in all of the changes at which one might guess, the Church will find her essence afresh and with full conviction in that which was always at her center: faith in the triune God, in Jesus Christ, the Son of God made man, in the presence of the Spirit until the end of the world. In faith and prayer she will again recognize the sacraments as the worship of God and not as a subject for liturgical scholarship.

Father Ratzinger's words are as true today as the day he spoke them. They reveal a profound and powerful insight — namely, that the Church will discover herself anew and be reborn a simpler and more spiritual reality. Indeed, just as the greatest sin brought about a singular act of redemption, so too will today's crisis be the catalyst to a purified Church, for every crisis offers both obstacles and opportunities. In this we see the cross and the Resurrection reflected in our own time, entering into the drama of our own lives and calling us to an ever-deeper commitment to our vocation. Picking up this theme and reinforcing Ratzinger's insights, Pope Francis said, "It will be a Church that is more spiritual, poorer, and less political; a Church of the little ones."

In our own lifetime, we've already witnessed a smaller Church as a result of the influence of postmodernism and its chief characteristic, moral relativism. It's in the air we breathe and the water we drink, such that its effects are inescapable. It's in the media and in print. It's in our schools and institutions. This is not to suggest that the world was perfect in the past — far from it. It is, however, to assert that the Judeo-Christian principles of the past, the very principles that shaped our western culture, have been slowly and steadily eroded, having a negative impact on participation in the life of the Church. This is equally true of our Protestant brothers and sisters, as well as our

Jewish cousins. Beyond this, the impact of the Covid pandemic has diminished the numbers in the pews and those entering the Church. Consequently, the beginnings of Father Ratzinger's rather prophetic message have come true, beginning even during his own lifetime.

The good news here is precisely that: the Good News. Jesus promised that the gates of hell would not prevail against the Church (Mt 16:18), and that He would be with us until the end of time (Mt 28:20). Throughout her history, the Church has undergone numerous persecutions and, in many respects, our current situation may seem mild compared to the past. However, this perception belies a darker reality. Whereas in the past, particularly in the pre-Constantinian era, these attacks were more direct, the persecutions of today are more indirect. They impact the Body of Christ through what Pope Benedict called the "Dictatorship of Relativism," reflected in such issues as abortion, euthanasia, transgenderism, and human trafficking, to name a few.

In the midst of this and other more direct persecutions, all of the baptized are called to bear witness to the Faith. Here clergy, this is to say, bishops, priests, and deacons, by virtue of our sacred calling, play a vital role. We're called, in defense of the Gospel, to serve the faithful and, by our own lives, to reveal Christ who is both priest and deacon (See *Catechism of the Catholic Church*, 1534). Indeed, Jesus identifies himself as such when He says, "The Son of man also came not to be served [*diakonos*] but to serve, and to give his life as a ransom [*sacerdos*] for many" (Mk 10:45; Mt 20:28). He is deacon and priest *par excellence* such that, in Him and through us, the world may know authentic love as service grounded in sacrifice. The above cited passage, found identically in Mathew and Mark, is the Christological foundation for the call to unity among the clergy. Because of this, it's worth a brief analysis here.

In both Gospels, Jesus' words arise out of a debate as to

which of His apostles will sit at His right and His left when He comes in glory. Here, Jesus reminds them that they aren't to rule like the Gentiles, as tyrants who lord themselves over the people. Rather, the greatest among them are called to be servants of the rest. This is a radical departure from how leadership was exercised in the ancient world. Jesus proposes a new style of headship among those in authority by placing leaders at the service of the very people they lead. Their well-being is to come before his, and their needs should be fulfilled first.

The Meaning of Unity

Within the context of what would be considered a rather upside-down approach to leadership by both Jews and Gentiles alike, Jesus now inserts himself and His mission as the exemplar by identifying himself as the "Son of Man." This was one of Jesus' favorite titles for himself. Although it was well-known in the Old Testament as one who is a devout follower of God (Nm 23:19; Ps 8:4; ninety-three times in the Book of Ezekiel), it was used in a particular way in Daniel as a term describing a great Messianic figure (Dn 7:13). In all of these, it's expressed in the indefinite form, such as "a son of God" or "one like a son of God." Jesus, now applying the phrase to himself, uses it in the definite form, "the Son of God."

In grammar, an indefinite article (a, an) is placed before a noun when its identity is not known or when it applies generally to a group. Conversely, the definite article (the) is placed before a noun to indicate that the identity of the noun is known to the reader. Here, Jesus is drawing a direct connection between the phrase "Son of God" and himself, revealing that the Messianic prophecy found in Daniel would be revealed in Him.

Beyond this, it would be helpful to recall the biblical notion of "corporate personality." Corporate personality refers to a concept used to understand the way groups were perceived and treated as unified entities in ancient societies. It's a concept that helps explain how the actions of one individual or a representative few could impact an entire group, and how the group as a whole could be held responsible or liable for the deeds of its members. So, for example, when David defeated the Philistine giant Goliath, his victory was not seen merely as an individual triumph but as a victory for all of Israel over their enemies. David's victory was attributed to the nation as a whole (1 Sm 17).

In a similar way, the title Son of Man, along with the meaning it carries, although primarily applied to Jesus, is also corporately applied to His Church — those who will be with Him forever. With this foundation now laid and providing a contextual framework, Jesus now describes how His Messianic mission would be fulfilled, as *diakonos* and as *sacerdos* — as deacon and as priest. Thus these two dimensions of His identity, grounded in His salvific mission, become the basis for clerical unity.

In this book, *clerical unity* refers to the state of being joined or linked as a whole, involving a sense of oneness, cohesion, and harmony. It implies a way of living out our vocation undivided, forming a single, complete entity while maintaining, in integrity, each order's distinctive and particular contribution to the mission of the Church. Therefore, when bishops, priests, and deacons, either all or in part, come together to create a whole without divisions or fragmentation, there is a sense of unity. It denotes a cooperative and mutually supportive relationship within and between the grades, while at the same time respecting the hierarchical structure. Moreover, unity often involves working together in a complementary manner toward a common goal or purpose, with shared faith, grounded in love of God and neighbor. In short, clerical unity signifies the interconnectedness, collaboration, and shared purpose among bishops, priests, and deacons. Despite their distinctive roles, they form a unified ordained ministry committed to advancing the mission of the Church by serving the People of God while upholding the teachings and traditions of the Catholic Faith.

Having defined what we mean by *unity*, we would do well to distinguish between "true unity" and "false unity." These represent two very distinct concepts that are often conflated. The inability to distinguish between these two will undermine the desire to be one by Our Lord.

True unity, the unity expressed by Christ (Jn 17:21) refers to a state of togetherness characterized by genuine harmony, agreement, and mutual understanding among bishops, priests, and deacons. It involves a shared faith, common goals, and a sense of cohesion that stems from real consensus and collaboration. True unity tends to be sustainable over the long-term because it is built on a solid foundation of a common Catholic Faith and a common mission that flows from that Faith. It can withstand challenges and disagreements because there is a genuine commitment to working through differences. This approach to unity often leads to positive outcomes, as it allows bishops, priests, and deacons to harness their collective strengths and resources effectively. It promotes cooperation, creativity, and the achievement of shared objectives.

True unity requires being honest while, at the same time, exercising prudence in charity. This means that, in pursuit of genuine unity, conflict is inevitable. This conflict may seem to contradict the unity sought; however, this need not be the case. The desire for authentic unity assumes a lack thereof and the willingness to come to some level of agreement even knowing there may never be complete unanimity. Conflict is thus inevitable among those sincerely seeking unity. The issue, then, is not whether there will be conflict, but whether that conflict can be resolved in accord with our Faith.

In this book, I will present some observations that may rub some the wrong way. This would seem, on the surface, rather

counterproductive. Yet these observations seek to reveal points
of contention in an effort to identify and address the source
of disunity. For those who may find my observations at times
somewhat harsh and one-sided, I ask your patience and forgiveness in advance. I don't claim to bring a ready-made solution
in these pages, but rather to start a conversation — one which
doesn't seek who's right and who's wrong, but instead, where the
truth lies.

False unity, on the other hand, involves a superficial or il-
lusory agreement or togetherness. It may appear as if bishops,
priests, and deacons are working together, but in reality, there
may be hidden agendas, conflicts, dissent, or insincerity. This
flawed approach is expressed in the common phrase, "Go along
to get along." Consequently, differences may be suppressed or
ignored rather than acknowledged and addressed. Here, conflict
is avoided at all costs for fear of undermining unity. Although
there may be times where we need to agree to disagree, this must
be the rare exception and not the rule. What is needed here is
great charity, prudence, and perseverance. Without these, and
the grace that accompanies them, discussions can lead to underlying tensions that remain unresolved. False unity is thus frag-
ile because it lacks a strong foundation of genuine agreement
and shared values. It can easily fracture when disagreements or
challenges arise because there is little commitment to resolving
underlying issues. The inability to address differences or the
presence of hidden conflicts can hinder cooperation and the
achievement of a common mission in Christ.

His Grace Is Sufficient

Though we can read, to some extent, the signs of the times, we
cannot foretell the future, and so we're left to speculate. Still, as
helpful as this "reading" may be, unless it's sourced and interpreted in Christ, we rob it of its soul. We fail to take into ac-

count that the God who created us, redeemed us, and sanctified us has chosen to place us in this age, this particular culture, and this specific moment. He knew, before the dawn of time, that we would be present in the here-and-now, and His grace, along with our openness to that grace, will be sufficient to continue the mission of the Church regardless of the persecutions we face. Consequently, the answer for what the Church may look like in the future arises not simply out of a consideration of the *zeitgeist*, the spirit of our age, but in our very selves and in Divine Revelation.

Consider that, at least in our own lives, the only two constants between past, present, and future are God and our individual selves. To the extent that we seek intimate communion with Christ, allowing Him, through our vocations, to extend His redemptive touch, we're living fully in the present and implicitly preparing for the future by staying faithful in that very same present. This is to say that God, who knows us better than we know ourselves, also knows the future better than we can ever predict it. To be sure, we should engage our will and intellect in the light of faith, but it's His Church, and He loves her far more than we can. This means that, in His divine providence, He has a plan. Our participation in His plan is to be attentive to His still voice through the teachings of the Church and contemplative prayer so that, as the future unfolds, we unfold with it. In this way, we incarnate Christ, revealing His divine love. Indeed, He's made present particularly through bishops, priests, and deacons so that, through our example, we may inspire and embolden the laity to reveal the love of Christ in their respective vocations. Together, and through the power of the Holy Spirit, we reveal the whole Christ (*Christus Totus*) to a world in desperate need of His saving love.

Christus Totus is a theological concept associated with St. Augustine of Hippo. This notion is deeply rooted in Augustine's understanding of the relationship between Christ and the Church, as well as the concept of the Church as the "Body of Christ." For him, *Christus Totus* emphasized the unity between Christ and His Church, viewing them as inseparable entities. He believed that Christ is not only the head of the Church but also its Mystical Body, and that all baptized believers are incorporated into this Body. This concept can be traced back to various passages in the New Testament, including the writings of the apostle Paul, who frequently used the metaphor of the Church as a body with Christ as its head (1 Cor 12:12–27; Col 1:18).

Augustine understood the salvific work of Christ as not merely rooted in His own actions, but extending to, and actualized in, the mission of the Church as that mission is guided by the Holy Spirit. He viewed the Church as the continuation of Christ's presence on earth, perpetuating His ministry and spreading His teachings. This perspective emphasized the idea that the Church, as the Body of Christ, participates in Christ's redemptive mission and serves as a means of God's grace and salvation to the world.

Augustine's *Christus Totus* also underscores the importance of the Church as a community of believers. Just as different parts of a physical body are interconnected and dependent on one another, so too are the members of the Church interconnected in their shared faith and mission. This unity in diversity is a reflection of the unity of the Body of Christ (Rom 12:5; 1 Cor 10:17; 12:27; Eph 4:12).

Although this is extended to all members of the Church in a complementary fashion, given the focus of this book, we will concern ourselves primarily with those in holy orders, with a secondary consideration of the laity. These two expressions of unity are interrelated, as all of humanity is called to be united as one in Christ Jesus. Clerical unity, then, is simply the implication of Our Lord's command to be one (Jn 17:21) as specifically applied to those who share holy orders.

A Complementarity of Orders

If, in the living out of their ontological configurations, the episcopate, the presbyterate, and the diaconate together reveal something essential of Christ and His gift of salvation, then the three orders must find their unity in the very same Christ. This unity, if it's to be authentic, must be formed and strengthened from the inside out. In this respect, it can't be merely functional but must also be relational. Where human beings relate, things function. It's far too easy in the exercise of our ministry to merely go through the motions, never reaching beyond that which is most proximate (the thing we do) to the ones we serve (the people we encounter). This deprives the encounter of its meaning and, in the process, depersonalizes it.

Sadly, this same temptation exists, to a greater or lesser degree, in the way members of the clergy relate to one another. The reasons for this depersonalization among some in the clergy are many and varied. Although they are worth exploring in some detail, it's a topic for another work. Nonetheless, whatever the reasons are, whatever the pathology, the remedy is always the same: Jesus Christ. He's the source of all unity and, with human effort transformed by grace, bishops, priests, and deacons can break down the functionalism that has invaded our ecclesial space and grow in communion with one another in Christ. This is His will for us, and this is how we grow in holiness.

Though this book will primarily focus on the unity between the grades of holy orders, much of what is written can also be applied to unity within these same grades. The decline in the number of priests has led to them becoming more and more separated from one another. This is particularly true of diocesan priests, many of whom live in isolation despite residing not far from one another. Although this parochial independence might be preferred by many, the lack of priestly community isn't

healthy. Unless priests actively pursue alternate ways to interact and share their lives with one another, they run the risk of
shrinking their priesthood to their particular experiences rather
than stretching themselves, uncomfortably at times, for the good
of those they serve.

In a similar way, deacons also need community and the unity it fosters. They need to interact with other deacons sharing
their lives and ministry. Many deacons exercise their ministry
in isolation from other deacons, even when they're assigned to
the same parish. Like ships that pass in the night, they see each
other, exchange niceties and a few ministerial notes, and then
they're off to whatever their assignment entails. Although most
of these deacons are married, their marriage cannot replace the
diaconal community they need. Just as priests need priests, deacons need deacons.

Although this unity is the personal responsibility of each
cleric by virtue of the faith they share and the order they received,
the chief responsibility for ensuring this unity falls to the bishop.
If he doesn't actively pursue unity within his diocese by creating
and fostering the structures for priests and deacons to gather
and interact, clerical unity will be significantly diminished and,
with it, the mission of the Church as that mission is exercised in
his diocese. This requires that the bishop not view his clergy as
a mere means to an end, as an extension of his pastoral ministry
among the laity, but as real coworkers in the vineyard, labor-
ing side-by-side and shoulder-to-shoulder. He needs to lay out a
clear and consistent vision of unity as a priority, and he needs to
share, in tangible and powerful ways, that vision with his clergy,
such that, motivated by the Spirit and inspired by his witness,
they fulfill their mission more effectively.

I suspect that some reading this will be struck with a certain
cynicism. Buffeted by the many scandals that have plagued the
Church over the last few decades, and the equally scandalous

manner in which these scandals have been dealt with by some bishops, it's easy to just blow off the idea of clerical unity as a pipe dream advanced by the naïve. Although in no way discounting the problems that have afflicted the Church, and in no way diminishing their negative effects, it would be a diabolical masterstroke to believe that grace can't overcome these challenges, no matter how severe. That's because the depths of evil and sin can't prevail over the heights of God's grace and mercy. Therefore, the move toward greater unity among the clergy isn't simply a good idea, but part of the very essence of our vocation. It calls us to love one another as Christ loved the Church, in a way proper to our vocation and state in life. Love of Christ, love of neighbor, and, more specifically, love of our brothers in holy orders, obliges us to move toward greater unity.

This essential concept underlies this book, as expressed in its title, *As I Have Loved You* (Jn 13:34). This unity, if it's grounded in a divine love, has a profound impact on our ability to bear witness to Christ so that others may believe. Recall the words of Our Lord just before His passion, when He said, "that they may all be one; even as you, Father, are in me, and I in you, that they also may be in us, so that the world may believe that you have sent me" (Jn 17:21).

External Change Arises out of Internal Transformation

Returning to our earlier consideration of the call to engage a changing world, I'm convinced that the response rests not so much outside of ourselves, but first and foremost within and among us. It lies within us through growth in the interior life, and among us by actively seeking unity between our clergy brothers, particularly those assigned by our bishops to labor in the same vineyard. Although we can distinguish between these two, we can't separate them, as they are two parts of the same whole, inextricably linked in Christ Jesus. Progress in the interior life is severely diminished without progress in unity. Likewise, progress in unity is equally diminished without progress in the interior life. These are corollaries of the Greatest Commandment (Mt 22:36–40), in that love of God is cultivated in the spiritual life and love of neighbor is realized in unity. Indeed, just as it's impossible to really love God without love of neighbor, it's equally impossible to grow in intimate communion with Jesus without growing closer to those around us. Recall the words of Our Lord when He said, "As you did it to one of the least of these my brethren, you did it to me" (Mt 25:40). It's this unity, sourced in the love of God, that imbues the ministry of bishops, priests, and deacons with the necessary quality to be salvific not only for those they serve, but for themselves as well.

The link between the interior life and unity among the clergy marks the unique approach to this book as expressed and realized in the RIM Dynamic. As we will later explore in detail, the RIM Dynamic is a process that emphasizes moving from the interior life to the exterior life, creating a stronger connection between spirituality and morality. This approach presupposes, as a first principle, that it's the will of God that clergy exercise their ministry side-by-side in a brotherly communion grounded in a filial love of the Father. This communion, if it's truly authentic, can't be passively assumed, but must be actively sought. The active seeking of the Christ in one another, regardless of how difficult it might be, requires significant work — work which some clerics may find unnecessary or even objectionable. As difficult as this might seem, however, it's part and parcel of Christian discipleship for, as Jesus reminds us, "If any man would come after me, let him deny himself and take up his cross daily and follow me" (Lk 9:23). Beyond this, we can be assured that, just as grace is available to take up our crosses despite the difficulties involved, so too will it be available to grow closer to our clergy brothers despite similar difficulties.

Communion and Mission

Communion between bishops, priests, and deacons is essential to the mission of the Church. In fact, the relationship between communion and mission is a central theological theme, especially articulated in documents like *Lumen Gentium*.

Understanding this relationship helps to provide insight into the nature and purpose of the Church herself. Indeed, Saint John Paul II's teachings echoed and expanded upon the ideas of *Lumen Gentium*, stressing the Church's dual nature as communion and mission. He emphasized that the Church's unity and communion are not ends in themselves but serve as the foundation for her mission to spread the Gospel and bring the saving love of Christ to the world.

The concept of communion as it relates to the clergy refers to the unity of all grades of holy orders, where all members are connected through ordination and their shared faith in Jesus Christ. This communion is not just a passive unity but an active participation in the life of the Church. When members of the clergy come together in communion, they strengthen each other's faith, support one another in their spiritual journeys, and collectively form a vibrant and dynamic community.

This sense of communion is essential for the Church's mission because a united and spiritually strong clergy is better equipped to carry out the task of evangelization and service. A clergy that is deeply connected in faith and love can effectively spread the Gospel message and engage in acts of charity and justice, incarnating in their words and actions the redemptive power of Jesus Christ.

On the other hand, the mission of the Church, which involves proclaiming the Gospel and serving humanity, has the potential to deepen the sense of communion among the clergy.

When bishops, priests, and deacons actively engage in mission in a coordinated way, they share a common purpose and vision. This shared mission unites them across different backgrounds and experiences, strengthening their bonds and fostering a deeper sense of belonging to the Body of Christ.

Additionally, engaging in mission can lead to personal growth and spiritual transformation. As the clergy step out of their comfort zones to share their faith and serve others, they often experience a deepening of their relationship with God and a greater appreciation for their fellow believers. This, in turn, enhances the overall sense of communion within the Church.

In short, communion and mission are intertwined in a reciprocal relationship within the context of the Church. Communion strengthens the Church's mission by providing a solid foundation of faith and unity, enabling effective outreach and service. At the same time, the mission of the Church deepens communion by uniting the clergy in a common purpose and fostering personal growth and spiritual enrichment. Together, these concepts reflect the dynamic and holistic nature of the Church's identity and purpose.

Purpose and Scope

The purpose of this book is to foster greater unity among the clergy, fulfilling the will of God as it is revealed in the mystery of salvation and realized in the mission of the Church. To accomplish this, it's specifically written to provide a way for bishops, priests, and deacons to explore, support, and strengthen their relationships as they seek to serve the laity in their respective vocations. This book is meant to be rather concise, consisting of five short chapters broken down into two broad sections. Where the first section lays the theological foundations, the second examines the pastoral and practical implications. This last section will also provide a means to personally and prayerfully reflect on the theological foundations, considering their impact and in-fluence on the interior life along with their implications on the exterior life. Beyond this, it will also provide an opportunity for clergy to share their insights with one another so that, aided by grace, they might grow in unity. In this respect, this book can be read alone, in a group, or some combination of both.

Chapter 1, "The Unity of Holy Orders," considers more thor-oughly the Christological dimension of holy orders as being sourced in the one Christ to whom all of the clergy are config-ured by virtue of their ordination, each according to his partic-ular grade. This establishes not only the fundamental starting point for our study but its ultimate end, intimate communion with Him. Central to this approach is a scriptural passage we've already touched upon and will continually unpack: that of Christ's own self-identification as deacon and priest (see Mt 20:28; Mk 10:45).

Chapter 2, "The Origins of Holy Orders as the Basis of Uni-ty," examines how this sacrament arises as a natural consequence of the paschal mystery. Through the use of Pope St. John Paul II's personalism, it provides an organic and systematic under-standing of the mystery of salvation as expressed in the mission of the Church. Here, the three grades of holy orders are under-stood in a complementary way while maintaining the hierarchy so that, together with the laity, they reveal the *Christus Totus*. This is accomplished by a profound participation in a singular act of divine love that's both received and passed on so that the entire Church "incarnates" Christ, each member according to his own state and vocation in life.

Chapter 3, "Discovering a Diaconate in the Priesthood," ex-plores the theological significance of the Church's requirement that a man first be ordained a deacon before he's ordained a priest. Beyond the historic adoption of the Roman *cursus hon-orum*, our consideration examines the intrinsic Christological connection between service and sacrifice, between *diakonos* and *sacerdos*. It describes how the ontological configurations of both the diaconate and the priesthood cohabitate in the sacerdotal orders and the significance of this cohabitation to the priest's identity and mission. The chapter concludes with the observation that one way to renew the priesthood, and to foster greater unity with the diaconate, is for priests and bishops to rediscover their own diaconate by being intentionally diaconal in the exercise of their episcopal or priestly ministry.

Chapter 4, "Discovering a Priesthood in the Diaconate," considers how deacons, in their own particular way, participate in the one priesthood of Christ. This unique participation, like that of the laity, though quite different from the ministerial priesthood, reveals a quality of sacrifice within the exercise of sacred ecclesial service — a quality unique to the diaconate. In this respect, the deacon pours himself out in his ministry such that his service now becomes a sacrifice and, because he offers it in union with Christ's own sacrifice, he becomes both priest and victim, albeit in a particularly diaconal sense. To better substantiate this priesthood within the diaconate, we return to the *mandatum* as understood within the context of the paschal mystery and ground it in the typology of Isaiah's Suffering Servant. Here again, we see how sacrifice (priesthood) and service (diaconate), as revealed in Christ, are inextricably linked to form a complementary revelation essential to the economy of salvation and the mission of the Church.

Chapter 5, "Relationship, Identity, and Mission," describes one of the most effective ways in which greater unity among the clergy can be achieved. Known by the acronym RIM, it provides an ongoing, three-step method that attempts to transform interpersonal relationships from the inside out, moving from the interior life to the exterior life. Here, with grace and persistence, the "two lives," so to speak, though quite distinct, become almost one, much as the soul permeates and penetrates the body. It's then through the body, this is to say our external actions, that unity is realized in the choices we make and the things we do. Drawn from the Institute of Priestly Formation (IPF) and modified for our purposes, it recognizes and seizes upon the essential factors necessary for unity among the clergy: Jesus Christ and the willingness of each participant to die to self.

Properly understood and practiced, RIM can provide the fundamental platform to strengthen the relationships among bishops, priests, and deacons, thereby positively impacting not only their ministry, but those they serve. As a result, the Church's mission is more effectively fulfilled and, in the very process, the participants grow in greater communion with God and one another. This chapter ends with a consideration of how those using this book in a group can continue meeting beyond this book so that they can grow in greater unity both personally and communally in Christ.

The appendix, "Spiritual Direction for Deacons," considers the spiritual care of deacons and the necessity of spiritual direction configured to their vocation. So that more priests may consider entering into this ministry for deacons, I've incorporated into this book a small text published by the Diocese of Phoenix, entitled *A Guide for the Spiritual Direction of Permanent Deacons*. This excellent publication was included with the approval of Bishop John P. Dolan of Phoenix. It's a concise, easy-to-read guide designed to help those spiritual directors or those discerning this ministry to more effectively direct deacons, along with aspirants/candidates in formation.

In my treatment of the diaconate and its relationship to bishops and priests, I will often place the deacon in a parochial situation. This is because nearly every deacon, even those whose primary ministry is extra-parochial, is assigned to a parish. This isn't to imply that the deacon is exclusively liturgical or parochial. Ministries of charity often find deacons in hospitals, prisons, nursing homes, or doing other corporal works of mercy. Instead, it's to describe where he most often relates to priests. In a similar way, although the wives of deacons play an important role in the deacon's ministry, the lack of reference to them and their role in this book is not meant to imply a diminished importance. This is equally true of the laity, as they are the beneficiaries and, in a manner proper to their vocations, sharers in the ministry of the clergy. Rather, the intent here is to maintain a tight focus on the relationship between bishops, priests, and deacons without excluding others.

A Two-Step Approach

As observed earlier, each chapter in this book is broken down into two distinct but related parts: the theological foundations and the practical implications. This is because, all too often, processes for achieving a specific end tend to reduce their methodology to the pragmatic alone. Like many secular books on marriage enrichment, they often focus on things the spouses can do, as though a change of actions in themselves is sufficient to bring about lasting transformation. In this respect, many of these well-meaning sources focus on the "what" and the "how" almost to the exclusion of the "why."

I suspect part of the reason for this external approach is that the "why," be it in marriage or the relationship between clergy, requires an inward search, recognizing that, for real change to take place and for that change to be sustained over time, interior attitudes must change first. To use a more theological term and apply it to our pursuit, the participants must be willing to undergo a *metanoia*. This involves not only the willingness to change our minds from an intellectual perspective, which is a lifelong process, but our hearts as well. If it's genuine, it will also involve ongoing self-examination, the recognition of our own sins and shortcomings, and the authentic desire to seek forgiveness from God and one another. Simply put, it requires a level of vulnerability and some personal sacrifice, without which change is merely superficial and passing.

In laying the theological foundations, I've attempted to draw my reader into the mind of the Church without getting too technical. Recognizing this, I will do my best to open up the mystery of God's love as revealed personally in our respective vocations and His desire that we become one. To accomplish this, I'll pitch the theological foundations at neither a popular level nor a scholarly level, but somewhere in between. My hope is to challenge my readers without losing them. Theological foundations, like those of our homes, aren't the most attractive part of the house. Nonetheless, they are absolutely necessary, if the house is to stand in the winds that blow and become a place to live in and thrive.

Often when we're introduced to new ideas and concepts, especially those of a spiritual nature, a single pass-through isn't enough. This means that what we discover in the initial encounter represents only a small part of an infinitely larger Truth, that is, God himself. Because this lesser truth is organically related to greater truths and ultimately to the Truth himself, it has the potential to unfold over time under the influence of the Holy Spirit. In this respect, what we have encountered so far, and what we shall encounter throughout this book, is seminal in nature.

Carrying the metaphor further, this means that, by tilling and fertilizing the soil, the seed has the very real potential to germinate and eventually bear fruit. In a similar way, through prayerful reflection, the theological truths we encounter in each chapter have the potential to reveal even greater truths. Consequently, if the reader desires more than just a cursory understanding of what he's read, and desires authentic unity among his clergy brothers, then a means is necessary to internalize the theological foundations of these truths such that, from them, the interior life is cultivated, authentic *metanoia* takes place, and genuine unity grows.

The practice of internalizing the theological foundations so as to bring about a specific *metanoia* will involve ongoing meditation and reflection before considering the practical and pastoral implications. So, in order to facilitate a second, more thorough pass-through of the material in each chapter, without being redundant, each chapter contains meditations and reflections. This section includes "Key Themes" and "Reflection Questions," both of which comprise a series of two integrated spiritual exercises: one focusing on prayerful meditation and the other on interior reflection. Together, these will allow for a deeper, more profound dive into the material, with the aim of internalizing and sharing it.

Applied to our goal, the meditations found at the end of each chapter provide a means to discover the "why" of our unity. This "why," when pursued seriously, automatically raises the question "how," as that "how" relates to our unique personalities and pastoral situations. Consequently, personal meditation is an essential first step to internalizing the theological foundations discussed earlier, both of which are necessary to the pursuit of unity. In order to tie the meditations directly into what was previously read, they are grounded in key themes extracted from the chapter. These themes are designed to reengage the reader with the material, enriching the earlier conversation by advancing it. It's precisely through this conversation — through this "back-and-forth," immersed in prayer — that the reader will appreciate more fully the "voice" of God and His call to be one.

As an integrated second step in this process, following the meditations, there are a series of three open-ended reflection questions. Each is specifically designed to offer a more in-depth, yet accessible, grasp of what was "heard" in the meditations. Although this method will be discussed in greater detail at the end of each chapter, the combination of meditations and reflections has the real potential to stimulate spiritual growth as that growth relates to clerical unity. All of this will require some work on the part of the reader, but rest assured, it's a work aided by grace which, in the end, finds its consolation in Christ. As Venerable Archbishop Fulton J. Sheen was quick to point out, "Whenever man attempts to do what he knows to be the Master's will, a power will be given him equal to the duty."

One final observation is necessary before we conclude this section. Our consideration of the relationship between priests and deacons assumes that holy orders is one single sacrament expressed in three grades: episcopate, presbyterate, and diaconate, having two distinct but related modes of participation: sacerdotal and diaconal (CCC 1536, 1554). Whereas the episcopate and presbyterate are sacerdotal in nature, the diaconate is diaconal. As first observed by Hippolytus of Rome in the third century, and reiterated by the Fathers of the Second Vatican Council, deacons are ordained *non ad sacerdotium sed ad ministerium episcopi*, that is, not to the priesthood but to the ministry of the bishop. For our purposes, because the episcopate and presbyterate share in ministerial priesthood, what is said in general of the presbyterate can also be said of the episcopate. Though we will later make certain distinctions between these two sacerdotal orders, and although we will discuss how both share in the diaconate by virtue of their earlier ordinations, everything applied to the presbyterate with respect to the diaconate pertains, in most respects, to the episcopate.

Exploring the Implications

As discussed earlier, this final section is designed to allow a deeper, more personal absorption of the material just covered. It consists of a set of two interrelated spiritual exercises, whose sole purpose is to reengage the key themes in this introduction so as to internalize the truths they contain. This is followed by a reflection on the pastoral implications of these same themes as they relate to greater unity among the clergy. For optimal results, this should take place in a two-step process, where the first step consists of a personal reflection, and the second consists of a communal sharing among clergy.

Recognizing that pastoral situations may differ, feel free to depart from this recommended process to suit your own particular needs. It is provided here to facilitate unity, not in any way to suggest there aren't better ways or that this is even the best way. In this regard, use what you want and modify it as you see fit. In all things be guided by the Holy Spirit, who desires our unity far more than we can, and whose grace is enough (2 Cor 12:9).

Step 1: Personal Reflection

The following represents some key themes found in the introduction. As you reflect on them, consider what Christ is revealing to you personally and your unity within the clergy. In this you're asking two distinct but related questions: "Lord, what are you saying to me *in general*?" and, flowing from this, "What are you saying specifically *to me* as I relate to my clerical brothers?" Ponder how what is said may impact your relationship to Him, and how this may influence your relationship with others, particularly in your attitudes and in the choices you make. As you meditate upon these things, write down your thoughts in your journal or spiritual notebook. This may be a single word, a sentence, a paragraph, or even more. The purpose here is to capture the most important elements of your meditation, even if they're not whole or complete.

Key Themes: As noted earlier, what's offered in these exercises is by way of fraternal recommendation. You're free to engage them as you see fit. Should you decide to move forward, you may take on one, some, or even all of the themes as the Spirit moves you. You may even wish to reflect and meditate on those themes within the introduction (and subsequent chapters) that are not provided on the list.

With this now in mind, the recommended key themes are as follows:

- The Church of the future is rooted in the present.
- His grace is sufficient.
- Consider the complementarity of orders.
- External change arises out of internal transformation.

Reflection Questions: Having meditated upon these themes and captured what Christ may be saying to you, you can further explore them in the following three reflection questions. In each chapter of this book, it is recommended that this be done in a separate sitting, giving you a chance to digest the fruits of your initial meditation. As with the key themes, write down your insights and thoughts in your journal or spiritual notebook.

- Identify and reflect on two or three things you learned from this introduction that you didn't know before, or now know better, regarding the unity of holy orders.
- Identify and reflect on two or three key spiritual insights you gained from this introduction that will help you in your life and ministry as a priest or deacon.
- Flowing from these insights, identify and reflect on two or three practical ways it might be possible to foster greater unity among your brother clerics in

your ministerial situation.

Step 2: Communal Sharing

The unity this book seeks to foster will be most effectively accomplished when the personal reflection is followed by a communal sharing. This should optimally occur in a small group setting in which all members, each having read the chapter and having done the reflection, now come together for an hour or so. This may take place in a parish setting, in which the pastor, parochial vicar(s), and deacon(s) initially commit to six regular meetings spaced two to four weeks apart. All six sessions, corresponding to the introduction and five chapters, should be scheduled at the beginning so calendars can be cleared and time set aside. A group leader should be selected to facilitate the discussion. This may be the pastor or someone he delegates. Beginning with prayer, the facilitator asks each member to summarize, in a time not to exceed several minutes, the following three reflections:

1. The two or three things he learned from this introduction that he didn't know before or now understands better regarding the unity of holy orders

2. The two or three key spiritual insights he gained from this introduction that will help him in his life and ministry as a priest or deacon

3. Flowing from these insights, the two or three practical ways it might be possible to foster better unity among his brother clerics in his ministerial situation

CHAPTER 1

THE UNITY OF
HOLY ORDERS

The importance of the sacramental life for any Catholic can't be overstated. Whether it's the sacraments of initiation, of healing, or of service, these have the very real potential to mediate an intimate encounter with God, imparting something of His divine life. Of course, in the Tradition, this is hardly new, as it has been expressed by the many saints, mystics, and Doctors of the Church.

In his work entitled *Tractates on the Gospel of John*, the great theologian and philosopher St. Augustine of Hippo emphasized the sacraments as visible signs of invisible realities, where human beings encounter the divine. Later, in the medieval period, St. Thomas Aquinas (the Angelic Doctor), in his various treatises on the sacraments found in his *Summa Theologiae*, consistently affirms sacraments as encounters with God. He views the sacraments as effective signs instituted by Christ himself to bestow divine grace upon the faithful. Aquinas's understanding of the sacraments, which strongly influenced the Tradition, particularly in and after the Council of Trent, reflects their essential role in facilitating a deeper, more intimate relationship between God and humanity, enabling the communication and reception of God's saving grace.

In a similar way, St. Francis de Sales, Doctor of the Church and spiritual father, wrote extensively on the interior life and the sacraments as encounters with God's love. In his *Introduction to the Devout Life* and *Treatise on the Love of God*, he highlights the sacraments as transformative encounters that deepen our relationship with God. Similarly, St. Teresa of Ávila, mystic and Doctor of the Church, explored the interior life and the sacraments as encounters with God's presence. In her *Interior Castle* and *The Way of Perfection*, she describes the sacraments as opportunities for intimate communion with God. Last, but certainly not least, St. John Henry Newman, theologian and great convert to the Faith, reflected on the sacraments as encounters with God's grace that transform. In his works, such as *Lectures on the Present Position of Catholics in England* and *Parochial and Plain Sermons*, he highlights the sacraments as moments of encounter that impart a participation in God's divine life.

As encounters with the living God that facilitate intimate communion, the sacraments also have a relational effect on the faithful in four ways. First, they create a bond with Christ. As noted above, by virtue of the encounter, the sacraments establish a profound union between the faithful and Christ. This is particularly true of baptism, where the faithful are incorporated into His Mystical Body, the Church. This bond with Christ deepens the relationship between the faithful and Our Lord, forming a spiritual union grounded in divine love.

Second, the sacraments facilitate and strengthen unity with the Church. Here, the sacraments also serve to bind individuals to the Catholic Church, the community of believers. The sacraments are always celebrated within the ecclesial and communal context. They are administered by the clergy, expressing and reinforcing the unity of the faithful with the Church. By receiving the sacraments, individuals enter into communion with the Church and become active participants in her life, worship, and mission.

Third, the sacraments facilitate communion among the faithful. Their celebration fosters a sense of communion and unity within the Church. This most often takes place in a communal setting, allowing individuals to join together in the worship and reception. Through shared sacramental experiences, individuals are supernaturally bound together as a community of believers, supporting and uplifting one another in their pilgrim journey.

Fourth, properly understood, the sacraments also entail moral obligations, leading to a virtuous and holy way of life. For instance, in the Sacrament of Baptism, individuals are called to live according to their baptismal promises, renouncing sin and embracing a life of holiness. In the Sacrament of Matrimony, couples are bound by the vows they make to each other and to God. In holy orders, bishops, priests, and deacons are ontologically configured to Christ in service to His Church. The sacraments, each in its own way, establish moral responsibilities and provide the grace necessary to live in accordance with the teachings of Christ and His Church.

By way of a summary, the sacraments bind individuals to Christ, the Church, and the faithful community. They establish a profound spiritual union, foster social unity, and impart moral obligations. Through the sacraments, we believe we're transformed and empowered to live out our faith in communion with God and our fellow believers. The sacramental life and, in particular, the vocations that arise out of these sacraments will provide a fundamental starting point for our discussion on the relationship between bishops, priests, and deacons.

Christ as the Source of Unity

Though, as we have just seen, all of the sacraments, to a greater or lesser degree, can be spoken of as relational, bishops, priests, and deacons realize this relationship in a particular way through holy orders. This is one single sacrament admitting of three distinct degrees, all of which participate in the fullness that is expressed and made visible by the episcopacy. This means that their unity is not so much derived from the fact that they partake in holy orders as such, or even in the diaconate in which they share, but the One to whom the sacrament points and makes present: Jesus Christ. Whether in the episcopate, presbyterate, or diaconate, all three are ontologically configured to Christ, each in his own way, such that He is made present in them. At the moment of their ordination, this configuration imparts an indelible character, which is a spiritual and supernatural quality now inherent in the soul. This, in turn, brings about a change on the deepest level of their being so that, well beyond the mission they share, well beyond whatever friendship they may or may not have, it is Christ who is the source of their unity.

To accept Christ as the source of our unity in holy orders isn't simply to recognize that we're called to grow closer to Him, as though He were only something external and transcendent. Indeed, because this initial transcendence was, in a limited sense, bridged by virtue of His Incarnation, God now dwells among us (Jn 1:14) and, if we allow Him, within us. This now makes possible intimate communion with Christ, in which we come to know Him, love Him, and serve Him in ever-deepening and more profound ways throughout our lives. In this respect, the source of our unity is not just to move toward Him as though He is far off, but rather to dwell within Him because He is already close at hand. It's to accept the invitation to intimately participate in His own life, not simply as one among many, but personally and uniquely.

This is what the saints and mystics meant when they spoke of the spiritual life. It is a life in which our interiority merges with Christ's own interiority, enabling us to experience a little bit of heaven on earth. In this encounter we discover and continue to discover the One who came "not to be served but to serve [*diakonos*], and to give his life as a ransom [*sacerdos*] for many" (Mk 10:45). As we've already seen, in this one statement, Jesus identifies himself as the deacon *par excellence* and the priest *par excellence*, in whom all deacons and priests find their identity, measure, and exemplar.

Because Christ is both priest and deacon, and because holy orders finds its unity within Him, to act against this unity, either by omission or commission, is to act against Christ himself, for He says, "As you did it to one of the least of these my brethren, you did it to me" (Mt 25:40). Therefore, for the sake of the Church's mission, for the sake of our own salvation, we are obliged to actively work toward the unity within holy orders, for it is there we encounter the God who loved us into being and, when we sinned, died for us.

This unity, arising out of our configuration to Christ, enables those ordained to act in His Person, the priest *in persona Christi Capitis* and the deacon *in persona Christi Servi*, thereby revealing, along with the laity, the *Christus Totus*. This, in turn, enables and empowers priests and deacons to realize and fulfill the Church's mission in their own lives and in the lives of others.

The implications of this dual fulfillment and the dynamic it expresses can't be overstated. The priest and deacon, in the exercise of their respective ministries, don't simply fulfill this mission externally as though it's merely something they do, but rather, from the inside-out as someone they are. Because they can't give what they don't possess (*nemo dat quod non habet*), without ongoing conversion along with intentionally living out their vocation, they're unable to effectively bear witness to Him as priest and deacon. This is why the interior life is inextricably linked to our ministry and the relationships among our clergy brothers.

The Primacy of the Interior Life

Ours is not so much an outward search for God but a desire to discover Him from within. The God who created us, who loved us into being, who died for us while we were still sinners, is already present in the interior life, waiting patiently to be encountered and reencountered. Although He's certainly present in the world around us — in the people we meet, in the situations we confront — that outward presence goes largely unnoticed, and is unappreciated, without an inward recognition. Our ability to see Christ in those we serve begins with an interior life attuned to His Divine Presence.

It's only in the interior life where we come to know and love the Christ to whom we were configured on the day of our ordination. As expressed succinctly in the first lesson of the Baltimore Catechism, knowing and loving are absolute preconditions for serving Him. This is because we simply can't love whom we don't know. Knowing isn't merely to understand God — to the extent possible — on an intellectual level through the study of faith, though this is essential. Without exposure to and immersion in such sources as the Scriptures, Tradition, and the Magisterium, we couldn't speak the Name of Christ, much less know Him. However, to truly know Him is to move in, through, and beyond this study (which is a lifetime endeavor) to a deep, interpersonal relationship, sharing in His very life. This is only possible through the cultivation of the interior life.

Relationships, if they are healthy, are always mutual. This is to say that they admit of a kind of reciprocity that ought to grow in intimacy and tenderness over time. In deepening our relationship with God through perfection in the spiritual life, we come, ever-so-slowly at first, to see ourselves as God sees us, albeit in a limited way. This wonderous self-revelation enables us to begin to appreciate our real self-worth. We are, as Jesus demonstrated so beautifully on the cross, someone worth dying for. Entering into this truth helps us to see that everything we have, every event we experience, be they triumphs or tragedies, are gifts from God.

When we prayerfully reflect on these gifts, when we meditate upon their implications, we discover in and through them the Giver — we encounter none other than God himself. These gifts are, in many respects, sacramental. They enable us, in a certain sense, to transcend the material world to reach the spiritual and there abide in His saving presence. Here, as we bask in the light of His love, we're overwhelmed by the encounter and experience a profound sense of gratitude. "Lord, I am not worthy to have you come under my roof" (Mt 8:8).

It's precisely this gratitude, born of our participation in divine love, that is the inspiration and motivation for ordained ministry. Thus the source of the bishop's episcopacy, the priest's priesthood, and the deacon's diaconate, that which enables each of them to effectively incarnate Christ in a manner proper to his particular vocation and order, is nothing other than intimate communion with Him. This communion is essential and absolutely necessary. In this respect, the interior life represents the place of inward encounter with Christ, without which a man is blind to the many exterior encounters with Christ that come his way each day. This inward encounter is what transforms the works a bishop, priest, and deacon perform from social work to ecclesial ministry — from a good thing to a saving reality.

In its broadest sense, the interior life is that inner place where we're alone with ourselves. It's the place of thought, imagination, deliberation, and choice. It's where we dream, pray, reflect, and meditate. It's where we discover God, ourselves, and others. It's the inner space where truth is grasped, goodness is acquired, beauty is appreciated, and love is born.

It's certainly possible, with some reflection, to distinguish between the various dimensions of the interior life. There's the speculative, capable of intellectual thought; the moral, capable of choosing good or evil; and the spiritual, capable of intimacy with God and others. These, of course, are interrelated and, in a certain sense, interpenetrate one another, finding their nexus in our one person. Although they can be distinguished by their operations, they can't be separated without somehow obscuring the whole person.

Although the interior life admits of these dimensions, when we speak of it, we tend to speak of the spiritual dimension. Because of this, terms such as *interiority, the inner life,* and *the spiritual life* are often used synonymously in the Church's Tradition. For our purposes, we will follow this usage, with all of these terms referring to that inner place where we encounter Christ and seek intimate communion with Him.

The interior life is immaterial and, because of this, finds its exercises within the powers of the soul. To be human is to be a body-soul composite, and whereas the soul expresses the interior life, the body expresses the exterior life. These two aspects of our human nature are to be integrated. This integrity requires that, for the interior life to be authentically lived, it must be expressed in the exterior life. This is nothing less than a corollary of faith and works. Accordingly, Saint James writes:

> What does it profit, my brethren, if a man says he has faith but has not works? Can his faith save him? If a brother or sister is poorly clothed and in lack of daily food, and one of you says to them, "Go in peace, be warmed and filled," without giving them the things needed for the body, what does it profit? So faith by it-

self, if it has no works, is dead. For as the body apart from the spirit is dead, so faith apart from works is dead. (James 2:14–17, 26)

Faith is an act of the interior life. For it to be realized and lived, it must be expressed in concrete acts consistent with what is professed. To do otherwise is to undermine its authenticity, calling into question whether that faith is truly held by the one professing it. Thus if someone were to profess to be a faithful Catholic while, at the same time, being unfaithful to his wife, his profession of faith would be significantly undercut by his actions. Indeed, those actions that are inconsistent with his Faith would call into question whether he truly believes what he says he believes. He may deceive others, and even himself, but this inconsistency reveals not his fidelity but his infidelity. Beyond this, if he freely and willingly engages in what he knows to be grave matter, he breaks communion with God and His Church. This is hardly the act of a faithful Catholic.

In many respects, the relationship between the interior and exterior life is sacramental. Properly understood, a sacramental, like the sacraments themselves, is a visible sign of invisible realities. The sign points to and makes present that which is hidden. Just as the body is the sacrament of the soul, the exterior life is a sacrament of the interior life. Without the body, the soul remains unknown, trapped in the realm of the spirit. It's precisely in and through the body that the soul enters the world and makes itself known and, equally important, comes to be known. Together, and only together, do body and soul express the whole person. In a similar manner, without the exterior life, the interior remains unknown and hidden. It's exclusively in and through the exterior life that the interior life is revealed. Together, and only together, do they express the whole person.

To share such things as faith and spirituality, hopes and aspirations — indeed, our very selves in love — the interior life must transcend itself. This only takes place through the exterior life, expressed in concrete acts. Likewise, to receive another's faith and spirituality, hopes and aspirations — indeed, their very selves in love — only occurs first through our exterior life. Our interior life is only accessed through the exterior life. This intrinsic relationship means that, although we can explore the spirituality of the diaconate, we do so with the understanding that, like faith and works, the interior life without the exterior life is dead.

With regard to the unity of holy orders, if this unity doesn't exist within the interiority of bishops, priests, and deacons, it won't exist externally across these grades. This is why it's necessary that the grades of holy orders that progress from the lower grade to a higher grade must never lose sight of the lower order to more fully realize the grace of the higher order. These orders are interdependent precisely because they find their one nexus in Christ and because the Christ encountered in the spiritual life is one.

This oneness gives rise to a final observation, that of "need," a term that should be understood as an exception, not a rule. Nonetheless, as an exception, it's important to identify it so that, when it occurs, and in the pursuit of unity, it can be addressed.

It's not unusual to hear from some bishops and priests that they don't need deacons. This most often results from a utilitarian understanding of the diaconate in terms of picking up some of the pastoral shortfall that may occur as a result of the declining number of priests. In this functional model of the diaconate, deacons are only valued based on the need as perceived by a particular bishop or priest. When, as in the case of an aging pastor, the deacon can provide the priest with help proper to his diaconate, he is valued. Conversely, when a young and more vigorous pastor is assigned and that help is no longer needed, then, assuming this functional model, the deacon's value is diminished and his contribution to the faithful is curtailed. It must be emphasized that this is the exception, not the rule. Still, it does exist, and where it exists, it's highly problematic. As Pope Francis observes:

> The decrease in the number of priests has led to a prevailing engagement of deacons to substitute them in tasks which, however important, do not constitute the specific nature of the diaconate. They are substitute tasks. The council, after speaking of service to the People of God "in the diaconate of the liturgy, of the word and of charity," emphasizes that deacons are above all … "dedicated to duties of charity and of administration" (*Lumen Gentium,* 29).

Although it's certainly true that deacons, by virtue of their ordination, can assist their pastors in ways the laity cannot, understood from a utilitarian perspective alone, this reduces the deacon from a person to be respected, acting in the person of Christ the Servant, to a thing that can be used. Despite the reality that this approach is more the exception than the rule, it does exist because it roots "need" in the subjective sense and fails to appreciate it in the objective sense as revealed by God. As a result, when we consider "need" as it relates to the diaconate, it must be done in the light of Divine Revelation as taught by the Church.

The need for the diaconate arises out of the deacon's unique contribution as bringing something that neither the bishop nor the priest does, Christ the Servant in a preeminent way, thereby making Him present by his life and ministry. This, as we shall see shortly, as expressed in the Establishment Hypothesis, grounds the whole of holy orders in the paschal mystery and, more specifically, in Christ himself.

In this respect, a deacon is needed in every ministry not because the bishop or priest believes he's needed, but because Our Lord himself has expressed this need in and through the ministry of the Church. Indeed, it's the Church, the one who speaks for Christ, that determines the need. To fail to recognize this fundamental truth is to fail to recognize Christ the Servant, and because the priesthood and the diaconate find their source and origin in Christ, they adopt a Christological dualism, obscuring in the very process the revelation of Our Lord and its salvific power. This is precisely why the interior life is so essential to the unity of holy orders, without which the orders remain isolated and their influence upon the laity diminished.

Thus it's the Church herself, as grounded in Divine Revelation, that determines the need for diaconal ministry, the need for Christ the Servant — not the pastor, not even the bishop. In my role as director of a large diaconate program, I regularly get calls from pastors who want a deacon assigned to their parish because of the workload. Although no deacon can replace a priest, he can, within the scope of his diaconal ministry, make up some of the pastoral shortfall, bringing some much-needed relief to the pastor. Although this can certainly be helpful, if the pastor fails to recognize the deacon's unique role and does not prioritize his duties according to that role, the deacon risks being reduced to merely a practical substitute for the pastor.

Exploring the Implications

As explained in the introduction, the concluding segment of each chapter will aim to offer a more profound and personal assimilation of the recently covered material. It comprises a pair of interlinking spiritual exercises with the sole intention of revisiting the central themes discussed in the chapter, thereby internalizing the truths they express.

Step 1: Personal Reflection
Key Themes:

- The four ways sacraments, as encounters with God, facilitate an intimate communion with Him and one another
- Christ the source of unity within the clergy
- The relationship between our interior and exterior life as these relate to clerical unity

Reflection Questions:

- Identify and reflect on two or three things you learned from this chapter that you didn't know before, or now know better, regarding the unity of holy orders.
- Identify and reflect on two or three key spiritual insights you gained from this chapter that will help you in your life and ministry as a priest or deacon.
- Flowing from these insights, identify and reflect on two or three practical ways it might be possible to foster better unity among your brother clerics in your ministerial situation.

Step 2: Communal Sharing
Refer to the "Communal Sharing" section at the end of the introduction on page 44 to complete this step.

CHAPTER 2

THE ORIGINS OF HOLY ORDERS AS THE BASIS OF UNITY

Earlier I spoke of the unity of holy orders in Christ. This unity, which finds its deepest meaning in Him, is also reflected in His life and ministry, particularly in the paschal mystery, His passion, death, resurrection, and ascension. A careful look at this mystery and, more specifically, the origins of holy orders, will expand our understanding of this unity as it relates to the mission of the Church.

Although much has been written on the origins of holy orders, it has tended to focus almost exclusively on the priesthood to the exclusion of the diaconate. However, as the *Catechism of the Catholic Church* points out, holy orders is a single sacrament consisting of three degrees (1536). If one degree, say the diaconate, is theologically impoverished, then the unity of holy orders suffers from this same deficiency. Put another way, the triune nature of this sacrament means that its unity is dependent upon the three degrees and their relationship to one another.

Commenting on this dependency, the English Dominican scholar Aidan Nichols observes, "The priesthood can't be approached in isolation from the episcopate and the diaconate." To better illustrate the relationship of the three degrees to the unity of holy orders, he goes on to observe: "To the ordinary Catholic Christian, the priesthood is the order with which he or she is most familiar, and understandably so. ... In this sense, it's the central image of the triptych: yet the central panel can't be appreciated without those which flank it. We need the whole picture."

The image of the triptych to describe the unity and diversity of holy orders is quite useful. As a work of art consisting of three hinged panels, the central panel serves as the focal point, depicting the main subject, whereas the side panels feature related scenes, figures, or symbols. When the side panels are closed, they hide the central panel, and when opened, they reveal the whole story. Using this same image and extending it, if one of the panels, say that of the diaconate, were only partially open, then the triptych would only disclose part of its truth, concealing something of the artist's intention. Moreover, this concealment not only obscures the one partially closed panel but, insofar as that panel hides part of the central panel, it obscures it as well. As a result, something of the message is lost.

For the entire truth to be realized, for the triptych to reveal the whole story, the side panels need to be extended. Without this full extension, we're left with an incomplete and partially disintegrated story. The same can be said of holy orders. Without the diaconal panel extended, we are left with an incomplete and partially disintegrated sacrament. In this case, something of the episcopate and presbyterate remain hidden and, beyond these, something of Christ himself. This is because each degree ontologically configures the ordinand to Christ in a way proper to the order received. In this respect, they incarnate Him in a preeminent way such that all three degrees, like the open triptych, reveal Christ in a way no single degree does. Indeed, because "holy orders is the sacrament through which the mission entrusted by Christ to His apostles continues to be exercised in the Church until the end of time" (CCC 1536), it plays a central part in the mystery of salvation. Consequently, "opening the tryptic wider" only serves to provide a more complete revelation of Christ, enabling the Church to more effectively fulfill her mission (Mt 28:18–20).

Observe also that the three panels only tell the whole story when they are hinged together and opened wide. The hinges are a figurative way of describing how the three panels relate to each other and how, together, they reveal the larger picture. Applying this analogy to holy orders, we would do well to focus primarily on the hinges: that which unites the three degrees as a means to discover a more integrated and complete theology of unity. In this respect, although we have recognized the deficiency of the diaconate as an example of a partially closed panel, our main concern lies in the whole of holy orders from which, like the priesthood, diaconal theology can be more effectively addressed at a later time.

One of the challenges in our consideration of the origins of holy orders is that, although the Church has treated this topic within her Tradition, the lack of a theology of the diaconate meant that it was incomplete. She most certainly has a strong understanding of the beginnings of the priesthood and a somewhat less developed but still substantial sense of the episcopacy. Nonetheless, theological explanations for the diaconate, as we've already observed, have been largely deficient. However, some recent strides in diaconal theology now make it possible to offer a more comprehensive understanding of the origins of holy orders and its unity. This new approach reveals not only the complementary relationship among bishops, priests, and deacons, but the complementary relationship between the clergy and laity in God's plan of salvation.

While writing my first book, *In the Person of Christ the Servant*, I quite providentially stumbled upon a way in which the Church might better describe the unity of holy orders. Using the personalist thought of Pope St. John Paul II, I discovered the philosophical language that would provide the ability to grasp more clearly the meaning of Christian service as it relates to the diaconate and indeed the whole of the Church. For those unfamiliar with theological development, talk of philosophical language may seem somewhat strange and out of place. However, in the Catholic Tradition, philosophy is considered the handmaid of theology (*ancilla theologiae*), with greats such as St. Augustine of Hippo relying on the thought of Neoplatonists, and St. Thomas Aquinas employing the work of Aristotle.

Non-Christian ways of speaking are often borrowed, modified, and applied anew to tease out a truth already present. In much the same way a nonbeliever can become a believer through baptism, philosophical language can be "baptized," so to speak, sanctifying its use. Thus, for example, Saint Thomas was able to describe the Real Presence of Christ in the Eucharist more clearly by using Aristotle's metaphysics (see CCC 1413). Similarly, Pope St. John Paul II used personalist philosophy in a great many of his teachings. Taking his work, I've applied it to the diaconate, revealing new insights, insights previously hidden and now made known — the most fascinating of which is service as a "gift of self." Here, diaconal ministry, or even the ministry associated with the episcopate and priesthood for that matter, is not so much something we do, but rather, someone we give, our very selves.

This insight is as profound as it is simple, moving the language of the diaconate away from a depersonalized function to an interpersonal reality. In serving others, it's not so much that I do something extrinsic and apart from myself, but rather that I, in the very doing of that something, give an intrinsic part of myself. I pour myself out to the very person I serve as a free gift, just as Christ did on the cross, in which I'm following His example. This imbues Christian service with a particular quality, such that it's not so much what I do, but how I do what I do. St. Francis Xavier understood this when he said, "It is not the actual physical exertion that counts toward a man's progress, nor the nature of the task, but the spirit of faith with which it is undertaken." This spirit of faith is not simply the Faith of the Church, but rather, the Faith of the Church as that Faith infuses me, transforms me, and motivates me to love others. It's precisely because of this Faith, through grace, that I am capacitated to gift myself to another in an authentically Christian way.

Of course, not all gifts are equal. Married deacons don't gift themselves to their parishioners or friends the same way they might gift themselves to their spouses and children. The nature of the relationship determines the kind of gift and the degree to which it's given. Where marriage, by nature of the sacramental love it possesses, requires the highest kind and degree of love for another human, the gift of self to God is in a completely different category. Unlike spouses, God, the First Giver, has given us everything. As a result, our response-gift to Him must be our all, total and complete. Indeed, because of a fallen yet redeemed human nature, this requires grace and a lifetime of effort on our part. Thus we can speak of our response-gift as a dynamic that, over time, has the potential to grow or diminish depending on our willingness to give.

As we shall see later, these gifts we make of ourselves, these acts of love expressed in ministry, be it priestly or diaconal, don't represent a zero-sum game. This is to say that the gift I give to one doesn't, by that very fact, decrease the gift I give to another.

In reality, quite the opposite is true. In gifting myself selflessly to another, my capacity to give myself to others increases. I become, in that act, a more giving person, imbuing my ministry with the quality of divine love, of salvific love, thereby revealing Christ. This requires a certain intentionality in the giving, a certain interior conscious act of the will to offer myself without expecting anything in return.

To appreciate what I mean here, consider the opposite. As you've no doubt experienced, it's quite possible to "pray" without actually praying, to serve or celebrate Mass without actually serving or celebrating. Though in this case, the grace is still given objectively *ex opera operato*, it's diminished in the deacon and priest *ex opera operantis*. This is because it's not sufficient simply to go through the actions on the outside without going through a corresponding set of actions on the inside (in philosophy, these inner actions are called "intentionality"). An approach that consists only of going through the motions empties the act of its authentic meaning because, regardless of the nature of the relationship, lack of intentionality results in only giving part of what is required. In this respect, such action is lacking in both justice and charity to God and the ones being served, rendering the act void of its natural end.

This gift of self, which is simply another way of speaking about love, intrigued me, especially as it is played out in the paschal mystery. As a result, by applying Pope St. John Paul's personalist thought, I not only had the language needed to better describe diaconal service but, quite providentially, I also had the language to better describe the unity of holy orders, both of which reveal and exemplify an authentic servant spirituality. It was while reflecting on this insight that I discovered what I would come to call the "Establishment Hypothesis." This will be discussed in greater detail as we proceed, but for now it's enough to say that the Establishment Hypothesis situates holy orders and

Christian service within the context of a human love sourced in divine love. This kind of love is only possible if we continually grow in intimate communion with Our Lord. St. Catherine of Siena, attributing these words to God speaking to her, beautifully illustrates the relationship between love of God and love of neighbor in ministry: "If you have received my love sincerely, without any self-interest, you will quench the thirst of your love for your neighbor just as sincerely. If someone fills their vessel at the fountain and then drinks from it, the vessel becomes empty. But if they keep their vessel in the fountain while drinking, it will always remain full."

Three Principles

The Establishment Hypothesis is grounded in three fundamental principles. The first and most important of these is the centrality of the paschal mystery. Indeed, as described in the *Compendium of the Catechism of the Catholic Church,* "The Paschal Mystery of Jesus, which comprises his passion, death, resurrection, and glorification, stands at the center of the Christian faith because God's saving plan was accomplished once for all by the redemptive death of his Son Jesus Christ." This, of course, is the core belief of all Christians and an essential doctrine of the Catholic Church. Simply put, the paschal mystery is what makes Christian doctrine authentically Christian. It's only in this mystery, which is the revelation of Christ himself, that holy orders find its fullest meaning and deepest expression.

Second, this redemption is offered by God, through His Church, by way of holy orders. Hence, as we've already seen, it is precisely through this sacrament that the mission entrusted by Christ to His apostles continues to be exercised in the Church until the end of time (CCC 1536). Holy orders then is not a human construct but a divine institution. It is, like the very Church it serves, "a plan born in the Father's heart" (CCC 759) and revealed progressively in history. Consequently, by the will of God, without holy orders — without bishops, priests, and deacons — Christ's saving mission would have ceased at His ascension. Of this, St. Ignatius of Antioch, writing to the Trallians, taught: "Everyone must show the deacons respect. They represent Jesus Christ, just as the bishop has the role of the Father, and the presbyters are like God's council and an apostolic band. You cannot have a church without these. I am sure that you agree with me in this."

In short, it's inconceivable for a Catholic to think of salvation outside the saving power of Christ's word and sacraments, which are dispensed to the faithful, historically and today, by those in holy orders.

Third, just as the paschal mystery is nothing less than a divine gift of self, an outpouring of divine love, so too it's perpetuated through a similar sacrificial gift of self in the three degrees of holy orders. This understanding of love, as noted earlier, was, for me, radical and revolutionary. To be sure, I understood love within the Catholic Tradition as willing the happiness of the other for the sake of the other; however, this new understanding of love as a sacrificial gift-of-self moves love from a desire of the will to concrete acts, which was implied in the Tradition, but not fleshed out in the same way.

Put another way, the quality of love is expressed in the depths of the sacrifice. Where there is no sacrifice, at least on some level, there is no love, only sentiment. This was the key contribution of Pope St. John Paul II to my thinking and, theologically, it made complete sense, advancing the Tradition to a whole new level. Christ's entire earthly life, from His Incarnation through His passion, death, resurrection, ascension, and future coming is nothing less than a sacrificial gift of self. This gift of self, unlike all others, is absolutely unique and utterly unrepeatable because it's a singular act of divine love, which is unconditional and knows no limits.

Nowhere is this gift of self more vividly expressed than in the crucifixion, where Our Lord gifts himself to all of humanity for all time. Jesus doesn't simply will our good in some sentimental or abstract way. Instead, He ensures that good by sacrificially offering himself to us in a concrete act of love that boggles the imagination. As beautifully expressed in the *Catechism*, "When the hour had come for him to fulfill the Father's plan of love, Jesus allows a glimpse of the boundless depth of his filial prayer, not only before he freely delivered himself up ... but even in *his last words* on the Cross, where prayer and the gift of self are but one" (2605).

God's plan of salvation, expressed most fully in the paschal mystery, is understood in a more profound way when it's interpreted as a series of successive gifts of self. Indeed, our ability to give ourselves, our ability to love others, begins with God's love (1 Jn 4:19), a love that is meant to be passed on. Because of this, we're called to love one another with a divine love, albeit in a human way (1 Jn 4:7); we're called to give ourselves in imitation of Christ. This is why the Fathers of the Second Vatican Council, influenced by Cardinal Karol Wojtyla (the future Pope John Paul II), taught that "man, who is the only creature on earth which God willed for itself, cannot fully find himself except through a sincere gift of himself."

All of this reveals that love, properly understood, isn't to remain the sole possession of the beloved. Like the man who buried his talents (Mt 25:14–30), we cannot bury the love we receive but instead must "invest" it in others. In this sense, the gift of self we receive is to be regifted. This means it is to be passed on to others and, through us, enable the love of God to spread. Jesus says, "A new commandment I give to you, that you love one another; even as I have loved you, that you also love one another" (Jn 13:34). Although the notion of self-gift as applied to sacrificial love emerges out of Saint John Paul's personalism, it has its roots in the Tradition. St. Augustine of Hippo, in his sermon on the martyrdom of Saint Lawrence, writes:

> As you have often heard, Lawrence was a deacon of the Church of Rome. There he ministered the sacred blood of Christ; there for the sake of Christ's name he poured out his own blood. … Just as he had partaken of a gift of self at the table of the Lord, so he prepared to offer such a gift. In his life he loved Christ; in his death he followed in his footsteps.

Thus, having received God's gift of self, we are to gift ourselves to others. In this respect, by divine providence, we incarnate God's love through our own flesh. Though we are unworthy, God allows us the privilege of actively participating in His plan of salvation. Applied to the Establishment Hypothesis (which will be treated more fully), this means that God's gift of self is successively passed on to the apostles, and through them to their successors, the bishops. The bishops then pass this gift of self on to priests and deacons, who themselves pass it on to the laity. The laity, having received this gift, now pass it on to the world (fig. 1). This is precisely how the mission of the Church is fulfilled and how the mystery of salvation unfolds.

Keeping these three principles in mind, and recalling the centrality of the Eucharist to holy orders, we now turn to the Establishment Hypothesis proper by considering the paschal mystery and its relationship to the Last Supper.

In many respects, the Last Supper isn't only part of the paschal mystery, it encapsulates it. This is to say that what Jesus said on Holy Thursday He actually did on Good Friday — "This is my body which is given for you" (Lk 22:19). This essential connection between the Last Supper and the paschal mystery is made explicit and reflected liturgically in the *anamnesis* in all of

A Series of Successive Gifts (fig. 1)

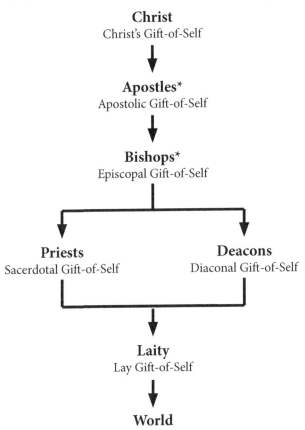

* Receives the fullness of the sacerdotal and diaconal gifts proper to their order.

the Eucharistic prayers. Indeed, by giving the command "Do this in remembrance of me" (1 Cor 11:24), He enables us to participate in the Last Supper and, by extension, the paschal mystery, each time Mass is celebrated. Accordingly, the *Catechism* teaches, "In the liturgy of the Church, it is principally his own Paschal Mystery that Christ signifies and makes present" (CCC 1085).

The Church has long looked to the Last Supper as the institution of the priesthood.

If, as we've already discussed, Christ as the *sacerdos* and the *diakonos* is the source of the unity of holy orders, and if He is most fully revealed in the paschal mystery as encapsulated in the Last Supper, then the Last Supper should be our starting point. Indeed, because the Eucharist was instituted at the Last Supper, this approach also allows us to maintain its centrality in our consideration. As elegantly expressed in the Second Vatican Council's *Sacrosanctum Concilium* (Constitution on the Sacred Liturgy):

> At the Last Supper, on the night when He was betrayed, our Saviour instituted the eucharistic sacrifice of His Body and Blood. He did this in order to perpetuate the sacrifice of the Cross throughout the centuries until He should come again, and so to entrust to His beloved spouse, the Church, a memorial of His death and resurrection: a sacrament of love, a sign of unity, a bond of charity, a paschal banquet in which Christ is eaten, the mind is filled with grace, and a pledge of future glory is given to us.
>
> On the night before He died, Jesus shared the Passover meal with His apostles. There, He issued two distinct sets of commands. The first, as we've already seen, is found in the Synoptic Gospels and consists of "Take, eat. ... Drink of it. ... Do this in remembrance of Me" (Mt 26:17–30; Mk 14:12–26; Lk 22:7–39; 1 Cor 11:23–26). These are known as the "Institution Narratives" because they simultaneously institute the Eucharist and the priesthood. However, during that same meal, there was another command, one not found in the Synoptics but instead only in John's Gospel. There, Jesus, after

washing the feet of His disciples, said, "I have given you an example, that you also should do as I have done to you" (Jn 13:15). This command is liturgically known as the *mandatum*.

On Holy Thursday, the *Ceremonial of Bishops* calls for the bishop to begin the foot-washing by removing his chasuble, under which is his dalmatic. These vestments represent the layering of holy orders, as the bishop's ordination to the priesthood, and his subsequent ordination to the episcopacy, do not supplant his earlier ordination to the diaconate. While he is bishop, he is still deacon, and the rite he is about to enact is one of service — that is to say, diaconal.

Pope Francis, during this ritual, does not wear the dalmatic. Instead, after removing the chasuble, he modifies his priestly stole into a diaconal stole before washing the feet of the people. This is to say, he takes the stole from around his neck and refashions it to run over his left shoulder and across his chest, thus denoting a deacon. Pope Francis and the bishops do this because, while they are bishops, they still possess the diaconate, and there is something intuitively diaconal about this act. The same is true with priests who are first ordained deacons. In washing the feet, they're acting in a diaconal capacity, though they don't wear the underlying dalmatic nor reconfigure their stoles. Reiterating this fundamental truth regarding the permanence of the diaconate, Pope Benedict affirmed:

> Every priest continues being a deacon, and should always think of this dimension, because the Lord himself made himself our minister, our deacon. We can think of the gesture of the washing of the feet, with which he explicitly shows that the master, the Lord, acts as a deacon and wants those who follow him to be deacons, that

they fulfill this role for humanity, to the point that they also help to wash the dirtied feet of the men entrusted to us.

It's fascinating to note the correlation between the two sets of commands at the Last Supper as they relate to the priesthood and diaconate and the two elements found in the Greatest Commandment. They are, in many respects, different ways of talking about the same thing, thereby providing each with fuller meaning. Recall that, when the Pharisees sent a scholar of the law to test Jesus, he asked Him which of the Commandments is the greatest. Recognizing their deceit, Jesus instead summarizes the Ten Commandements by saying: "You shall love the Lord your God with all your heart, and with all your soul, and with all your mind. This is the great and first commandment. And a second is like it, You shall love your neighbor as yourself" (Mt 22:37–39: Mk 12:28–31; Lk 10:25–28; Jn 13:31–35).

According to the *Catechism*, "The Commandments take on their full meaning within the covenant" (2061). In its most basic sense, a covenant is a promissory agreement between God and humanity, either verbally or by ritual oath, that establishes a new relationship. Since the Fall (Gn 3:1–19), God has established a series of covenants with Israel as a means to slowly reconcile humanity to himself, ever deepening His relationship with us. These are known as the old covenants, corresponding to the Old Testament. These old covenants culminate and find their fullest expression in the redemptive act of Jesus Christ, who is the New and Eternal Covenant.

Whereas the Greatest Commandment represents a summary of the old covenant — love of God and love of neighbor — the Last Supper represents the new and everlasting covenant (Lk 22:20), grounded in the paschal mystery and memorialized in the celebration of the Mass. This is expressed in all of the Eucharistic prayers when the celebrant says, "Take this, all of you and drink from it, for this is the chalice of my blood, the blood of the new and eternal covenant, which will be poured out for you and for many for the forgiveness of sins. Do this in memory of me." At the Last Supper — and in the paschal mystery it encapsulates — both love of God and love of neighbor are expressed respectively in the Eucharist and *mandatum*. In the Eucharist, God offers His love to us through His Son Jesus Christ, making possible our ability to love Him with all our hearts, our souls, and our minds. In a similar manner, the *mandatum* calls us to love our neighbor through service: "You also should do as I have done to you" (Jn 13:15).

Returning to the Last Supper, in this one event, an event that takes up the whole of the paschal mystery, we have two sets of commands from Christ: One is unmistakably priestly, and the other is unmistakably diaconal. In this respect, the Establishment Hypothesis isn't really new. Deacon James Keating writes, "The foot washing scene at the Last Supper is an expression of the institution of the diaconate by Christ, since it reflects the doctrinal truth of the unity of Holy Orders. There is symmetry between the '*Do this* in memory of me' (Lk 22:19) charge to the apostles, and his other apostolic charge 'so that as I have done for you, *you should also do*' (Jn 13:14–15)." In making this claim, Keating cites Cardinal Walter Kasper, who asserts:

> We have seen that without *diakonia* there cannot be a Church, because Christ himself is one who serves (Lk 22:27). Therefore, at the Last Supper … he not only established the idea of priesthood, but, in principle, also laid the foundation of the diaconal ministry. By the washing of feet, he gave us an example, so that we also do, as he did to us (Jn 13:15). In these words, one can see

the foundation of the diaconate.

Where the Establishment Hypothesis breaks new ground, and where it builds upon Keating's and Kasper's intuitive observations, is that it describes precisely how this happens through a series of successive gifts of self (acts of love). Critical to this is the fundamental reality that we simply cannot give what we don't first possess. In other words, if the apostles hadn't received the fullness of what we now call "holy orders" from Christ, they couldn't have passed it on to the bishops. Likewise, if the bishops hadn't received holy orders from the apostles, they couldn't have passed it on to priests and deacons. In a similar fashion, if priests and deacons hadn't received their orders from the bishops, they couldn't have passed them on to the laity in the form of priestly and diaconal ministry. As we've already seen, this progression is grounded in the Latin maxim "*Nemo dat quod non habet.*" Simply put, they can't give what they don't have.

To better appreciate this progression as it relates to the unity of holy orders and the mystery of salvation, I'll break this process down into seven simple steps. In considering these steps, it's important to notice how each step is distinguished from the others by distinct gifts-of-self that form an integral and organic continuity. Critical to a correct understanding of this progression is that, following the example of Christ, what is given is not some*thing*, but instead some*one*. This is a key insight of personalism, moving ministry from a functional approach to an interpersonal and incarnational reality.

Within the progressive gift of self, it's also important to observe that God is the ultimate source. The subsequent gifts of self represent a ministerial sharing in what God has already bestowed on the minister. This is to say that the apostolic gift of self to the bishops is not so much the apostles' gift as though it's sourced in them alone. Rather, this gift originates with Christ and, through the grace of participation, flows through the hands of the apostles to the bishops. In a similar fashion, the subsequent gifts represent a passing on of a gift ultimately sourced in the Divine and received in a manner proper to the receiver. So, for example, the laity don't receive this gift so much from priests and deacons as though they are the source, but from Christ through the hands of the priest and deacon. In this respect, Christ's gift is not diminished at each level but distributed in a manner proper to the receiver, enabling the receiver to receive the fullness of that gift and, as a result, become an agent of that gift to others. In what follows, each step of the hypothesis will be discussed in relation to the diagram below (fig. 2).

- Step 1: Through His gift of self on the cross, Jesus reconciles humanity to the Father. This reconciliation, expressed in the paschal mystery, is encapsulated in the Last Supper, which is also a foretaste of the heavenly banquet to come.
- Step 2: In the Last Supper, Jesus issues two sets of commands to His apostles, one at the Eucharist, and the other at the *mandatum*.
- Step 3: These commands, in light of the paschal mystery, institute both the priesthood through the Eucharist and the diaconate through the *mandatum*. This constitutes Christ's gift of self to the apostles.
- Step 4: The apostles, having received this gift of self from Christ in both the priesthood and diaconate, now gift themselves to their successors, the bishops. This constitutes the apostolic gift of self to the episcopacy.
- Step 5: The bishops, having received a full share of Christ as both *sacerdos* and *diakonos* through the apostles, now pass this gift of self on to priests and

deacons in a way proper to their order: priests being configured to Christ the Priest, and deacons being configured to Christ the Servant. This constitutes the episcopal gift of self to priests and deacons.

- Step 6: Priests and deacons, having received a specific share of *sacerdos* and *diakonos*, each in a manner proper to their order, now pass this gift of self on to the laity in a manner proper to the lay state through evangelization, the dispensation of the sacraments, and acts of charity. This constitutes the priests' and deacons' gift of self to the laity.

- Step 7: Finally, the laity, having received this gift of *sacerdos* and *diakonos* in a manner proper to their vocation through baptism (CCC 1547), now pass it on to the world. This constitutes the lay gift of self to society.

The combined effect of this self-giving from Christ to the world (steps 1–7) manifests the *Christus Totus*. The use of this phrase may seem an overstatement, perhaps even hyperbole. However, it's employed here in a very limited and very specific sense. First, it does not imply that the process of self-giving expressed in the hypothesis reveals absolutely everything about Christ. This is obviously not true. Rather, it simply means that the fullness of God's Revelation in Christ is made known through the apostles and their successors under the guidance of the Holy Spirit. This Revelation is articulated and transmitted by the entire Church for the salvation of the world. Such an articulation also comprises everything that flows from it, including the Scriptures, the Tradition, and the Church's doctrinal, moral, sacramental, and liturgical life. Second, taken together and interpreted by the Magisterium, these sources provide the believer with all that is necessary for redemption in Christ. It's only in this limited and salvific sense that we can rightly speak of the *Christus Totus* as applied to the Establishment Hypothesis (see fig. 2 on page 78).

Establishment and Institution

> "Brethren, pick out from among you seven men of good repute, full of the Spirit and of wisdom, whom we may appoint to this duty. But we will devote ourselves to prayer and to the ministry of the word." And what they said pleased the whole multitude, and they chose Stephen, a man full of faith and of the Holy Spirit, and Philip, and Prochorus, and Nicanor, and Timon, and Parmenas, and Nicolaus, a proselyte of Antioch. (Acts 6:3–5)

Having demonstrated the connection between the origins and unity of holy orders as grounded in the Revelation of Christ and the mystery of salvation, one more thing is needed before we can proceed. It concerns how the Establishment Hypothesis, which claims to locate the origins of the diaconate in the paschal mystery, can be reconciled with how these same origins have been identified in the Tradition with Acts 6.

Catholic theology admits of a certain organic unity, and therefore it's not sufficient to offer a new way of thinking without showing how it "fits" with a prior way of thinking. Tradition has long recognized, and universally affirmed, the above Scripture passage as the origins of the diaconate. The event occurred after Jesus' ascension and therefore after the Last Supper. How then can we reconcile the institution of the seven men, as found in Acts 6:3–5, with the Establishment Hypothesis that places the origins of the diaconate in Christ's paschal mystery? Because it's grounded in Divine Revelation, the institution can't be dismissed, nor can it be diminished. It must,

The Establishment Hypothesis (fig. 2)

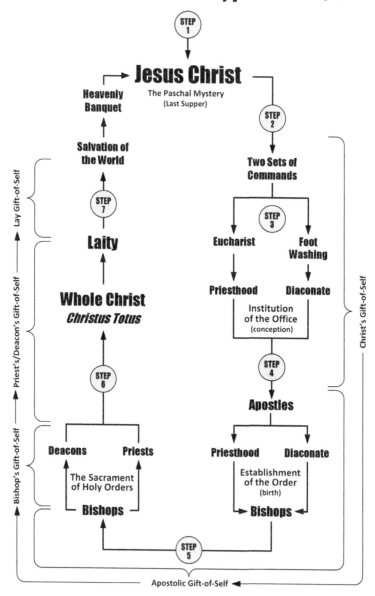

if the hypothesis is to maintain its integrity, be reconciled in some meaningful way, such that the institution of the Seven becomes an integral part of the hypothesis.

One way to address this apparent conflict is through the distinction between *officium* (office) and *ordo* (order). Whereas an office is a position in a larger organization that carries with it a specific function, an order is an office shared by two or more persons who, together, form a recognized body. Logically speaking, an office always precedes an order. So, for example, before someone can enter the order of bishops, there must first be an episcopal office. Similarly, before someone can enter the order of presbyters, there must first be the presbyteral office. Likewise, before someone can enter the order of deacons, there must first be a diaconal office. This distinction explains how it is possible that the *mandatum* at the Last Supper established the office of deacon, whereas the selection of the Seven and apostolic laying on of hands represents the institution of the diaconal order.

If this seems somewhat obscure, perhaps a simple biological analogy would be helpful. Let's consider the conception of a baby within his mother's womb, followed by his birth. Whereas an office represents a kind of conception, an order represents a kind of birth. Just as conception is the coming to be of someone, the *mandatum* is the coming to be of the diaconate. Likewise, just as birth is the outward revelation of a conception nine months earlier, so too is the institution of the Seven the outward revelation of the *mandatum*. Such an understanding reconciles the Establishment Hypothesis with the Church's traditional teaching about the diaconate, in much the same way as conception and birth are reconciled. They aren't two distinct things; rather, they are the growth of one thing looked at from two distinct stages of development. Such an approach lends a sense of continuity and trajectory that neither of the two do alone.

There is some implicit evidence for this process in the Scriptures. We know, for example, that the office of priesthood was established at the Last Supper. However, the presbyteral order was instituted sometime after, as witnessed by Luke (Acts 15:6, 23) and Peter (1 Pt 5:1). Likewise, we can say that the episcopal office (the fullness of orders) was also established at the Last Supper. However, the episcopal order was instituted sometime after, as witnessed by Paul's Letter to Timothy (1 Tm 3). If this is true of the presbyterate and episcopate, then it's reasonable to conclude that it's also true of the diaconate. Folding all three degrees of holy orders into the Establishment Hypothesis provides a clearer understanding of their unity, diversity, and complementarity, while at the same time grounding them together in the paschal mystery.

Christ's total gift of self means that the complementary relationships among the episcopacy, priesthood, and diaconate find their nexus in the one Person of Christ. Each order participates and contributes in a unique way to bringing, with the laity, the *Christus Totus* to the world. This means that, through the use of Pope St. John Paul II's personalist language, we have, for the first time, not only a new way of envisioning the origins of holy orders, but perhaps even more importantly, an organic way of speaking about the unity of holy orders and its impact on the mission of the Church.

If the above is true, and I believe that it is, then the diaconate isn't ancillary to God's plan of salvation, but is an absolutely integral and indispensable component. This in no way detracts from the episcopacy and presbyterate but complements these orders and enriches them. Although the diaconate, beginning in the fourth century, began a slow decline as a permanent order in the West, it was maintained in the East as a transitional order and continues up to the present. This means that the

Church was never without the diaconate in some form. The Second Vatican Council did not restore the diaconate as a permanent order because of the shortage of priests, as there was no shortage at the time of the council. Prophetically, I believe the council fathers restored the order because the future would require the presence of Christ the Servant in a preeminent way as an example to all of the faithful, laity and clergy alike, to gift themselves in salvific love to one another through acts of service. Recall again the words of Jesus just before His sacrifice, as He washed the feet of His apostles: "I have given you an example, that you also should do as I have done to you" (Jn 13:15).

Exploring the Implications

Step 1: Personal Reflection

Key Themes:
- The image of the triptych and how a deeper understanding of one order leads to a deeper understanding of the other two
- Love as a sacrificial gift of self given by Christ and passed on through the exercise of ordained ministry
- The Establishment Hypothesis as it relates to clerical unity, the mystery of salvation, and the mission of the Church

Reflection Questions:
- Identify and reflect on two or three things you learned from this chapter that you didn't know before, or now know better, regarding the unity of holy orders.
- Identify and reflect on two or three key spiritual insights you gained from this chapter that will help you in your life and ministry as a priest or deacon.
- Flowing from these insights, identify and reflect on

two or three practical ways it might be possible to foster better unity among your brother clerics in your ministerial situation.

Step 2: Communal Sharing
Refer to the "Communal Sharing" section at the end of the introduction on page 44 to complete this step.

CHAPTER 3

DISCOVERING A
DIACONATE IN THE
PRIESTHOOD

The diaconate is not a partial sacrament. To understand this, let's begin by asking a fundamental question. Why does the Church require that every priest, before he's ordained to the priesthood, must first be ordained to the diaconate? The historical answer to this question, at least in part, can be found in the adoption of the *cursus honorum*. This was the Roman practice whereby men advanced progressively from a lower to a higher political office. With respect to the grades of holy orders, this practice was adopted by the Church in the post-Constantinian era, in both the East and West, to provide sufficient and adequate clerical formation. As a result, a tradition developed where candidates for the priesthood would pass through a series of sequential orders culminating in ordination to the presbyterate over a designated period. It was during this time, beginning in the fourth century, that the diaconate as a "permanent" order slowly declined and became a "transitional" stage to the priesthood.

It's important to note that, despite the introduction of the seminary system by the Council of Trent in the sixteenth century, which standardized clerical formation, the diaconate remained a "stepping stone" to the presbyterate. Similarly, the practice of ordaining men as "transitional" deacons continued after the Second Vatican Council's restoration of the diaconate as a permanent order. Although some have suggested that this practice is no longer necessary, these suggestions have gone largely overlooked, implying that the Church still sees a certain value, perhaps even an essential value, in ordaining men to the diaconate prior to their ordination to the priesthood.

The designators "permanent" and "transitional," as applied to the diaconate, though practically helpful, are theologically problematic. Although it does distinguish deacons who are being prepared for the priesthood from deacons who aren't, the diaconate is one single grade of holy orders and, in this sense, isn't part of a sacrament but a particular participation, a diaconal participation in the sacrament proper. Thus, at diaconal ordination, the deacon receives not a partial sacrament, but a whole sacrament although, at the same time, not its fullness (something reserved exclusively to the episcopacy).

The same is true of the priesthood. Like the diaconate, the priesthood is one single grade of holy orders and, in this sense, isn't part of a sacrament but a priestly participation in the sacrament proper. Thus, at priestly ordination, the priest receives not a partial sacrament, but a whole sacrament although, at the same time, not its fullness. That said, and as we shall see, this presbyteral order complements the earlier diaconal order and does represent a fuller participation in holy orders. This is precisely what is meant when the Church calls this sacrament "holy orders" (plural). Although all three orders have an organic unity in the one sacrament, each possesses an integrity proper to itself such that each rightly bestows a sacrament. Consequently, within holy orders there are three grades within two modes of participation, *sacerdotal* and *diaconal*, the fullness of which is possessed by the episcopacy. In this way, one can properly speak of ordination to the diaconate as a sacrament, ordination to the priesthood as a sacrament, and ordination to the episcopacy as a sacrament without undermining the unity of the one sacrament of holy orders.

Even the vow of celibacy doesn't separate these grades, as unmarried candidates to the permanent diaconate must also take this vow, and married candidates to the priesthood under the pastoral provision need not. Indeed, the designator "permanent" is rather redundant, as the sacrament imparts an indelible character and is, by its very nature, permanent. Thus the terms *permanent* and *transitional* are simply ones of convenience, but this convenience comes at a cost, implying that the newly ordained priest is no longer a deacon. Indeed, it fosters the erroneous impression, particularly among the lay faithful, that the newly ordained priest now transitions out of his diaconate and into the priesthood. Although it is certainly true that he is now ontologically configured to Christ the Priest and, in this respect, he can now act *in persona Christi Capitis*, his diaconate, which is also ontological, possesses an equally indelible character, albeit different. The priesthood, though objectively a higher grade, does not swallow up his diaconate; rather, the two cohabitate in the one man. Accordingly, the USCCB's *Program of Priestly Formation* affirms: "The sacramental configuration to Christ the Servant was also conferred on the priest at his diaconate ordination. This configuration is not lost when he is ordained a priest but rather continues in imitation of Christ, who came not 'to be served but to serve and to give his life as a ransom for many.'"

Key to understanding these three participations is the notion of vocation. Each grade is not a level to which one climbs in order to reach a higher level as though a corporate ladder or military rank. Instead, it's a response to a gratuitous and personal call by God to uniquely participate in the mission of Jesus Christ. Although the episcopacy and presbyterate are objectively higher grades than the diaconate, the deacon with respect to the presbyterate, and the presbyterate with respect to the episcopacy, are not denied anything when they receive a lower grade. This is because each order is unmerited and a gratuitous gift, and each, from a subjective perspective, is complete and sufficient for the recipient. As with those deacons subsequently ordained to the presbyterate, and those priests subsequently ordained to the episcopacy, the earlier grade was complete and sufficient at the time of its reception. Now, having received the call to a higher office, they respond without in any way diminishing the call and ontological configuration of the lower office. In doing so, this further participation in holy orders means that, as we've already seen, they cohabitate in the one man in a complementary way.

Part of the challenge to this cohabitation and the mutual enrichment it provides to bishops and priests arises out of a minimalistic approach taken by many seminary formators. Other than part of a course on holy orders or liturgy, most seminary curriculums don't address the diaconate as such. As observed in a recent paper:

> As seminary formation and curriculum stand today, seminarians rarely encounter a robust theology of this grade of Holy Orders in their formation. Seminary theologians and formators are eager to "get to priesthood" in their classes and meditations. Locating preparatory diaconal ministry within the pastoral stage of priestly formation, as articulated by The Ratio, marks an occasion for seminaries to develop a more intentional theological formation in and spiritual experience of

diakonia itself. While seminarians live the diaconate's meaning in a parish setting, the seminary's theologians can be forming a true diaconal imagination within these future priests.

The lack of diaconal formation within priestly formation is, by any measure, a significant lacuna. Given its sacramental nature, to ignore or downplay sufficient preparation for this, or any sacrament for that matter, is to imply its lack of significance to the recipient, to the mission of the Church, and indeed to the mystery of salvation. Although all of the sacraments are efficacious, imparting a grace *ex opera operato*, the ability of the recipients to receive this grace *ex opera operantis* is significantly diminished by their lack of formation. Although the newly ordained, by virtue of the prayer of ordination and the laying on of hands, are fully deacons, their ability to appropriate their diaconate in a personal way and subsequently into their priesthood remains largely *in potentia*. This, coupled with the very short period between priestly and diaconal ordination, undercuts the essential value of the diaconate to the priesthood and serves to deepen the erroneous notion that the diaconate is nothing more than an intermediate and temporary stage to the priesthood. In this respect, the diaconate has virtually no significance beyond itself and no practical implications in the life of priests and bishops. It also has profound implications for how many bishops and priests view the diaconate and the diocesan resources, or lack thereof, given to diaconal formation and ministry.

Thus far we've examined some of the historical and formational reasons why the Church requires that every priest, before he's ordained to the priesthood, is ordained to the diaconate. Although important, these reasons are insufficient in themselves, as alone they do not address a potentially deeper theological reason, one not yet explored in the Tradition. Perhaps, with the help of personalism and advancements made in diaconal theology, it may be possible to open wider that particular panel of the tryptic, revealing not only something more about the diaconate but the priesthood and episcopacy as well. In doing so, we might better address the cohabitation of orders within the priesthood and episcopacy and its implications in the life of bishops and priests and, indeed, the Church as a whole.

The Irreducible

Bearing this in mind, another personalist theme will prove helpful here: that of the irreducible. In contrast to Thomistic anthropology where the person sits atop the continuum of being, personalism does not view the person as simply an object among other objects in the natural world differentiated by his will and intellect. Indeed, just as Saint John Paul II maintained that, by reflecting on human experience, certain truths emerge that give rise to a more complete understanding of the human person, the same can be said for its application to the cohabitation of holy orders in the one man.

Where the classical approach tends to reduce the person to the otherwise helpful Aristotelian-Thomistic categories, human experience reveals the entire person as a concrete whole. Consequently, although it's true that a person possesses, by his very nature, a body and soul, when we encounter him, we encounter him as a whole person. This fundamental revelation means that the person cannot be boiled down or reduced to objective classifications or functions, no matter how insightful these might be. To do so would be to examine the parts at the expense of the whole. Therefore, applied to holy orders, any consideration of Jesus, to whom the ordinand is ontologically configured, that reduces Him to general categories of being or functionality, passes over that which is most human. Indeed, it's precisely this human, in a sacramental sense, that points to and reveals the divine. It's in this respect that we can say a person is "irreducible."

To better appreciate the irreducible as it relates to the cohabitation of holy orders, we need to once again consider how, in describing His mission, Jesus defines himself as one who serves and gives himself up for others (Mt 20:28; Mk 10:45). In this one statement, as we've already seen, we have both *diakonos* and *sacerdos*. Indeed, these descriptors ground His mission in two distinct but interrelated activities and, based on the Latin maxim *"Agere sequitur esse"* ("To act is to follow being"), says something essential about Him. This fundamental truth is used to describe the link between what a person does and who he is, such that what he does flows directly from who he is. Put another way, his actions, especially those of great importance to him, emanate from his own sense of identity. Consequently, by examining one's actions, we can learn something about the person.

In this respect, Jesus is both *diakonos* (one who serves) and *sacerdos* (one who offers sacrifice and is sacrificed). Applied to the paschal mystery, in Jesus' passion, death, resurrection, and ascension, He gives himself irreducibly as both deacon and priest. He can give himself no other way, because both find their definitive meaning in Him. In other words, when Jesus gives himself for the salvation of the world, which is perpetuated in holy orders through the mission of the Church, He does so whole and entire. This is not to suggest that each grade of holy orders receives both *diakonos* and *sacerdos*. Where the deacon receives only a portion of Christ's own *diakonos*, the priest and the bishop, having already received Christ's *diakonos* in their diaconate, now receive a portion of Christ's own *sacerdos*, in a measure proper to their respective orders.

As long expressed in the theological tradition and affirmed by the Magisterium, each grade of orders, by a special grace of the Holy Spirit, configures the ordinand to Christ (CCC 1581). This configuration imparts an indelible spiritual character, be it episcopal, presbyteral, or diaconal (CCC 1582). Derived from the Greek word *charassein*, *character* describes an image or inscription engraved in a permanent way on a medal, coin, or piece of stone. In a certain sense, the reception of holy orders, like that of baptism and confirmation before it, leaves something behind like an impression. This "something," which St. Augustine of Hippo describes as the mark of the Lord, is so radical that it impacts the recipient on the deepest level and cannot be effaced.

Although this teaching is long established, the Magisterium and theological community have yet to describe how these orders cohabitate in the one man. By *cohabitate*, I mean abide and interact with one another such that the higher grade does not obliterate or even diminish the lower grade. This cohabitation is important not only to the lives of bishops and priests, but to the mission of the Church as that mission plays out in dioceses and parishes.

Of course, the cohabitation of character is hardly exclusive to the grades of holy orders. Both baptism and confirmation, each in its own way, also cohabitate in the one person. Moreover, once a man receives holy orders, these earlier sacraments continue to ontologically abide in him. If this cohabitation arises out of the divine will, and God never contradicts himself, then we must conclude that each application of sacramental character exists in a complementary fashion, such that they enhance or emphasize the qualities of each other.

In our consideration of this complementarity, perhaps it would be helpful to begin with the relationship between baptism and confirmation as a basis for our subsequent consideration of the relationship between the diaconate and priesthood. Although different and distinct sacraments, they each impart character (CCC 1272, 1304), and it's the interrelationship between characters that may provide some rich insights. Reflecting the sacramental tradition with regard to confirmation, the Church has long taught that, although distinct from baptism, the reception of confirmation "is necessary for the completion of baptismal grace. For 'by the sacrament of Confirmation, [the baptized] are more perfectly bound to the Church and are enriched with a special strength of the Holy Spirit. Hence they are, as true witnesses of Christ, more strictly obliged to spread and defend the faith by word and deed'" (CCC 1285).

In this case, the character imparted in confirmation abides alongside the character imparted in baptism such that each provides a specific grace while at the same time revealing something the other does not. This "joining," so to speak, doesn't efface or diminish the previous character, nor do they merge into some third thing, but instead they enrich each other with a quality that more fully strengthens and specifies the recipient for mission. The principal effects of baptism are purification from sin and a new birth in the Holy Spirit, incorporating the recipient into the Church; now cleansed and incorporated, the recipient of confirmation receives a fuller outpouring of the Holy Spirit to boldly bear witness to the Faith.

As a result, he's united to Christ and His Church more firmly and experiences an increase of the gifts of the Holy Spirit. Along with these effects, confirmation also "gives us a special strength of the Holy Spirit to spread and defend the faith by word and action as true witnesses of Christ, to confess the name of Christ boldly, and never to be ashamed of the Cross" (CCC 1303). In this respect, it provides the grace to uniquely participate more fully in the mission of the Church, maturing the recipient in faith.

In all of this, it's essential to bear in mind that each sacrament, though different and distinct, has one goal in mind: greater intimate communion with Christ Jesus. They are sacred encounters such that each sacrament orients the recipient to Our Lord in a particular way, enabling the recipient to participate in his own salvation (Phil 2:12–13). Among many things, we can conclude from this that both baptism and confirmation, as with the remaining five sacraments, find their nexus in Christ with the ultimate goal of eternal life with Him. If all of this is true of the cohabitation of character in baptism and confirmation, might it not be equally true of the grades of holy orders?

Indeed, if this is true, then the character received at priestly ordination no more effaces or diminishes the character of the diaconate ordination than the character received at episcopal ordination effaces or diminishes the character of priestly ordination. Instead, these grades, along with the character and grace they impart, abide and cohabitate in the one man such that they further strengthen and specify him for mission. At the same time, depending on the openness of the recipient, they provide ongoing opportunities to encounter Christ, grow in holiness, and participate in his own salvation. Thus, just as it would be unthinkable for a bishop to abandon or diminish his priestly identity at his episcopal ordination, it is equally unthinkable for a priest to abandon or diminish his diaconal identity at his ordination to the presbyterate. Indeed, if this happens with respect to the diaconate, then priests will fail to see Christ the Servant in their own ministry and, since bishops are drawn from that very same presbyterate, they too will fail to see this same Christ in the exercise of their own episcopal ministry.

Echoing this fundamental principle, Pope Francis, in an address to the transitional deacons of Rome, said:

> The diaconate does not disappear with priesthood: on the contrary, it is the foundation on which it is based. You will be priests in order to serve, conforming with Jesus who "came not to be served but to serve, and to give His life" (Mk 10:45). I would say, then, that there is an inner foundation of priesthood to be preserved, which we could call

"*diaconal conscience*": just as conscience underlies decisions, so the spirit of service underlies being a priest. So, every morning it is good to pray asking to know how to serve: "Lord, today help me to serve"; and every evening, giving thanks and making an examination of conscience, to say: "Lord, forgive me when I thought more of myself than of serving others." But to serve, dear friends, is a verb that refuses all abstraction: to serve means to be available, to renounce living according to one's own agenda, to be ready for God's surprises that manifest themselves through people, the unexpected, changes of plan, situations that do not fit into our schemes and the "rightness" of what one has studied.

This "diaconal conscience" can be metaphorically envisioned as concentric spheres, where the inner, more fundamental sphere offers structural and supportive underpinnings for the larger, outer spheres. This imagery illustrates how each sacramental character coexists and resides within the same individual, layered in significance and scope (fig. 3). In this case, the most fundamental sphere is that of baptism, as it now unites the recipient to Christ and is "the basis of the whole Christian life, the gateway to life in the Spirit … and the door which gives access to the other sacraments" (CCC 1213). Along with confirmation, these innermost spheres provide the structure and underlying support for the next sacrament that imparts character, the diaconate. Likewise, should the deacon advance to the priesthood, the diaconal sphere now gives structure and underlying support to the priestly sphere. Finally, should the priest advance to the episcopacy, the priestly "sphere" now gives structure and underlying support to the episcopal sphere. In each of these sacramental characters, there exists a necessary reliance and interdependence such that to diminish or ignore an earlier character is to significantly undermine those received later.

Bear in mind that here we are considering only the sacraments that impart character. The other four sacraments (Eucharist, reconciliation, anointing of the sick, and marriage) also confer different types of grace, including sanctifying grace, sacramental grace, actual grace, and special graces specific to each particular sacrament (see CCC 2000). Their absence in this analysis is in no way to diminish their necessary significance. It's only to underscore how the sacraments of character cohabitate in the one man.

The Cohabitation of Sacramental Character (fig. 3)

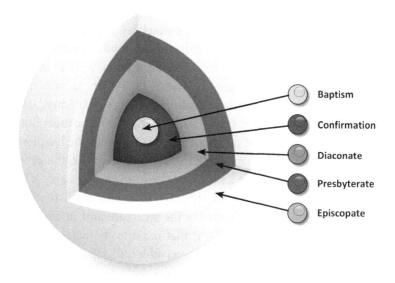

The image of the spheres gives rise to another related observation, that of rediscovery and appropriation. As illustrated above, if a man, after baptism and confirmation, were to pursue ordination of the diaconate, and if he has not progressed in his lay vocation by virtue of those earlier sacraments, then the underlying structure and support for the diaconate is insufficient for fully living out his diaconate. Put another way, the structure of the underlying Sacraments of Baptism and Confirmation lack the necessary structural integrity to support his diaconate. This, in turn, results in a weak deacon. The same is true with the priesthood and episcopacy.

The good news is that, even if one has an insufficient structure and support of the earlier sacraments, through grace and human effort, they can be rediscovered and re-fortified such that what was once insufficient now becomes sufficient. This is to say that the grace of the earlier sacraments that were received *ex opera operato* now can be appropriated more fully *ex opera operantis*. This means that the earlier grace given *in potentia* now becomes actualized in the person, enabling him to incarnate Christ through his vocation more effectively. With regard to the episcopacy and priesthood, this means an intentional and on-going appropriation of their diaconate such that it infuses their ministry with Christ the Servant.

With the above in mind, and returning to the question of why the Church requires that a man must first be a deacon before he becomes a priest, I believe the answer lies in Christ's own self-identification as deacon and priest (Mk 10:45). Based on Our Lord's example, as foreshadowed in Isaiah's Suffering Servant, service is essential to sacrifice, or, to use more ecclesial language, diaconate is essential to priesthood. To better demonstrate what I mean here, consider that the Greek word *diakonia* (literally meaning *service*), is translated into the Latin term *ministerium,* which itself is translated into the English term *ministry.* When we speak of "episcopal ministry," we're actually saying the *diakonia* of the bishop. Likewise, when we speak of "presbyteral ministry," we're actually saying the *diakonia* of the priest. This means that those sacramental functions associated with bishops and priests are inescapably diaconal in their expression. So, for example, the confection of the Eucharist, which is proper to the priesthood alone, is absolutely dependent upon the exercise of a particular service. Indeed, this *potestas sacra* remains completely hidden within the priest without its outward manifestation through a sacramental act, an act of *diakonia*. Thus the exercise of priestly ministry, although exclusive to the priesthood and episcopacy, is inescapably diaconal. The diaconal dimension is, in this way, necessary, but not sufficient. This means that, although sacerdotal ministry is diaconal, diaconal ministry is not sacerdotal, at least not in the same sense.

If the above is true, and I believe that it is, then, based on the Establishment Hypothesis and the cohabitation of holy orders, it's not theologically possible to ordain a man to the priesthood without first ordaining him to the diaconate, any more than it's possible to ordain a man to the episcopacy without first ordaining him to the priesthood. These orders, despite being distinct in themselves, are integral to one another and to the one sacrament, representing Christ to His Bride the Church. This suggests that what emerged as a discipline, arising from the adoption of the Roman *cursus honorum*, may have evolved into a doctrine. Understood this way, it experiences, like all doctrines, an organic development. Consequently, although in antiquity the Church practiced a *per saltum* approach (skipping some grades) to ordination, she shortly thereafter practiced a *per gradum* approach (each grade in order). This progression may represent an authentic development, such that what was implicit in the past now becomes explicit in the present.

All of this gives rise to a fascinating observation. Inasmuch as Christ unites, and inasmuch as each of the three grades of holy orders have been indelibly configured to Christ the Servant, Christ the Servant, as expressed in the diaconate, unites these grades. A brotherhood of fraternal service exists between bishops, priests, and deacons that has yet to be fully explored and can provide a means for greater unity within the clergy. This is precisely why, as we've seen earlier, Pope Benedict says, "Every priest continues being a deacon, and should always think of this dimension, because the Lord himself made himself our minister, our deacon." This unity, when intentionally fostered among priests and deacons, can have a positive impact on the pastoral life of the Church as she faces new challenges.

Finally, although this relationship of the diaconate within the priesthood has never been explicitly expressed in the doctrinal Tradition, it has, nonetheless, been expressed in the liturgical tradition *lex orandi, lex credendi*. According to this principle, that what the Church prays she believes, we see in the long practice of ordaining men first to the diaconate before priesthood something of what she implicitly believes. With the restoration of the permanent diaconate by the Second Vatican Council, along with such contributions as the Establishment Hypothesis and other developments, it's now possible to make what was previously implicit explicit, at least to some extent.

Exploring the Implications

Step 1: Personal Reflection
Key Themes:
- The lack of diaconal formation within priestly formation and its subsequent impact on the bishop's/ priest's relationship with their own diaconate, the diaconate in general, and deacons in particular
- Vocation as a call to Christ through His own irreducibility as priest and deacon
- The cohabitation of holy orders and the ability to rediscover and more fully appropriate the grace already received

Reflection Questions:
- Identify and reflect on two or three things you learned from this chapter that you didn't know before, or now know better, regarding the unity of holy orders.
- Identify and reflect on two or three key spiritual insights you gained from this chapter that will help you in your life and ministry as a priest or deacon.
- Flowing from these insights, identify and reflect on two or three practical ways it might be possible to foster better unity among your brother clerics in your ministerial situation.

Step 2: Communal Sharing
Refer to the "Communal Sharing" section at the end of the introduction on page 44 to complete this step.

CHAPTER 4

DISCOVERING A PRIESTHOOD IN THE DIACONATE

Just as the priesthood shares in the diaconate of Christ, so too does the diaconate share in the priesthood of that same Christ, though in a very different way. Where, by virtue of his earlier ordination to the diaconate, a priest is ontologically configured to Christ the Servant, the deacon is configured to the priesthood of Christ by virtue of his baptism, as his baptism is now shaped by his ordination to the diaconate. True, although all three grades of holy orders share in the diaconate, only the presbyterate and episcopate share in the ministerial priesthood. Still, if carefully nuanced, it's quite possible, and theologically accurate, to speak of the "priesthood of the diaconate" without in any way encroaching on the ministerial priesthood. Such an insight, as we shall see, has profound implications for the deacon and the Church he serves.

At first blush, it may seem odd to speak of the diaconate as participating in Christ's priesthood, because the Church sees these as separate and distinct orders. Although this distinction is essential and must be maintained to ensure the integrity of the three grades of holy orders, there's a certain sense in which the diaconate and presbyterate both participate in the one priesthood of Christ, each in their own way.

To better appreciate what I mean here, consider the teaching that there are two participations in the one priesthood of Christ: the common priesthood and the ministerial priesthood. The common priesthood, sometimes called the priesthood of the laity or royal priesthood, arises out of baptism. For those ordained to the presbyterate, this common priesthood is further specified and ontologically enriched by ordination to the ministerial priesthood. Accordingly, the *Catechism* teaches:

> The ministerial or hierarchical priesthood of bishops and priests, and the common priesthood of all the faithful participate, "each in its own proper way, in the one priesthood of Christ." While being "ordered one to another," they differ essentially. In what sense? While the common priesthood of the faithful is exercised by the unfolding of baptismal grace — a life of faith, hope, and charity, a life according to the Spirit — the ministerial priesthood is at the service of the common priesthood. It is directed at the unfolding of the baptismal grace of all Christians. (1547)

It's interesting to observe that as the common priesthood is not swallowed up by the ministerial priesthood, the Church considers the two as separate and distinct from each other. The move from one kind of participation to the other occurs at ordination, indicating that holy orders impacts how participation in the one priesthood of Christ is lived out. If this is true, and if deacons receive holy orders, isn't it reasonable to conclude that there may well be a hitherto undiscovered third participation in the one priesthood of Christ: a diaconal participation? If not, then the diaconate is the only segment of the faithful that doesn't partake of Christ's priesthood, as deacons, once they become deacons, are no longer counted among the laity. Although there's no formal teaching on the matter of diaconal participation, this form of diaconal priesthood has not gone unnoticed. Accordingly, Saint John Paul II acknowledged this diaconal participation when, in his catechesis on the diaconate, he taught:

> The catechesis I have given on the diaconate, in order to complete the picture of the ecclesiastical hierarchy, thus highlights what is most important in this Order, as in those of the presbyterate and the episcopate: a specific spiritual participation in the priesthood of Christ and the commitment to a life in conformity to him by the action of the Holy Spirit. … Deacons, therefore, are called to participate in the mystery of the cross, to share in the Church's sufferings, [and] to endure the hostility she encounters, in union with Christ the Redeemer. It is this painful aspect of the deacon's service that makes it most fruitful.

Here, John Paul indicates that there is, in fact, a unique diaconal participation in the one priesthood of Christ. Insofar as a priest is one who offers sacrifice, the deacon's gift of self in the exercise of his ministry can be, and should be, a gift that takes on the form of sacrifice. This means that the exercise of the deacon's diaconate can never be reduced to doing something, even if that something is holy. Such a form of ministry can become cold and depersonalized when it's reduced to a mere mechanical act. Instead, diaconal ministry is not so much something the deacon does, but someone he gives — his very self.

This moves ministry away from a purely functional approach to a relational approach, where the deacon connects person to person, soul to soul. This not only makes Christ the Servant present but, because Christ is one, He makes visible the invisible Crucified and Risen Lord.

A consequence of this reality is that no one should be chosen as a deacon on the basis of what he has done or is doing, but rather on the basis of how he has "lived" what he is doing or has done. The diaconate is not a medal to reward the most visibly active lay person, but a configuration to Christ the Servant that enables him to serve more deeply in the presence of the Father.

Before moving on, and having earlier looked at the participation of the diaconate in the priesthood and, more specifically, how the laity participate in the one priesthood of Christ, it would be instructive to touch upon how the laity participates in the one *diakonia* of Christ, thereby completing the picture. To this end it's possible to take the language previously used by the *Catechism* (1547) regarding the priesthood and modify it to speak about the diaconate. In this respect, it could be said:

> The ministerial or hierarchical diaconate, and the common diaconate of all the faithful, participate, each in its own proper way, in the one diaconate of Christ. While being ordered one to another, they differ essentially. In what sense? While the common diaconate of the faithful is exercised by the unfolding of baptismal grace — a life of faith, hope, and charity, a life according to the Spirit — the ministerial diaconate is at the service of the common diaconate. It is directed at the unfolding of the baptismal grace of all Christians. The ministerial diaconate is a means by which Christ unceasingly builds up and serves His Church.

In Search of a Typology

One way to better appreciate the priesthood of the diaconate is to revisit the connection between service and sacrifice as expressed in our earlier treatment of the Establishment Hypothesis. Recall how we demonstrated that both the priesthood and the diaconate were instituted at the paschal mystery as revealed and memorialized in the Last Supper. Whereas the Eucharist instituted the priesthood, the *mandatum* instituted the diaconate. Both find their nexus in the one Christ and in that one redemptive act. To facilitate our treatment of the connection between service and sacrifice, we would do well to examine certain biblical typologies.

In its most basic sense, a typology is a method of interpretation that involves recognizing certain elements, characters, events, or institutions in the Old Testament (type) as foreshadowing or prefiguring corresponding elements, characters, events, or institutions in the New Testament (antitype). This approach acknowledges that there are meaningful connections between the Old and New Testaments, where the earlier elements are seen as providing insights into the later ones.

Typology goes beyond mere coincidence or similarity; it's grounded in the belief that God's plan and purpose are revealed through these connections. Typological relationships highlight the unity and continuity of God's Revelation across both the Old and New Testaments, showing how God's plan unfolded and reached its fulfillment in Jesus Christ and the Church.

With regard to the diaconate, the Church, through the writings of St. Ignatius of Antioch, St. John Chrysostom, St. Augustine of Hippo, St. Ambrose of Milan, and St. Gregory the Great, has long recognized the Levites as being the type of the diaconate. In the Old Testament, the Levites were descendants of Levi, one of the twelve sons of Jacob. They were distinct from the other tribes, as they were called by God to serve in the tabernacle and later in the Temple. They were given responsibilities that revolved around the sacred rituals, maintaining the sacred spaces, and facilitating worship.

The Levites were not priests in the traditional sense, but their role was crucial in connecting the people with the divine. They assisted the priests, who were descendants of Aaron, another son of Levi, in performing sacrifices, maintaining the sanctuary, and offering prayers on behalf of the people. The Levites acted as intermediaries between the people and the priesthood, ensuring that the worship of God was conducted in a fitting and reverent manner.

Centuries passed, and a new era dawned with the coming of Jesus Christ. In the heart of the New Covenant, the Church was established by Christ as the continuation of God's plan for salvation. Just as the Levites served as intermediaries between the people and the priesthood in the Old Covenant, a distinct order of clergy emerged within the Church: the deacons.

These deacons, inspired by the Levitical service, took up a role of service and ministry that echoed the Levites' responsibilities. Like the Levites, deacons were not ordained to the priesthood but were set apart for a specific ministry within the Church. They became a bridge between the laity and the priests, aiding in various practical aspects of Church life, such as liturgy, charitable works, pastoral care, and the distribution of the Eucharist.

The relationship between the Levites and priests of the Old Testament draws intriguing parallels with the dynamic between deacons and priests in the Church today. Just as the Levites supported the priests in the sacred duties of worship, deacons today assist priests in ministering to the faithful. The Levites' focus on service and maintaining the sanctuaries finds resonance in the diaconate's emphasis on practical and charitable ministries.

Similarly, the relationship between priests and deacons echoes that of the priests and Levites. Just as the priests in the Old Testament held a distinct "sacramental" role and a deeper engagement with worship, the priests in the Church administer the sacraments and lead the community in worship. Deacons, on the other hand, play a supporting and necessary role, complementing the priests' ministry with their diaconal ministry.

Both pairs — Levites/priests and deacons/priests — embody a collaborative effort to ensure the flourishing of worship and the well-being of the community. Just as the Levites foreshadowed the diaconate, their close connection with the priesthood serves as a reminder of the unity within the clerical ranks. This typological relationship, spanning centuries and covenants, underscores the continuous thread of God's plan and His use of distinct roles to enrich the life of His people.

Although the typology of the Levites/deacons does provide some insight to the connection between service and sacrifice, it does not directly link it to a diaconal participation in the one priesthood of Christ. However, if we extend our reflection of the *mandatum*, it should be possible to discover a typology of a diaconal participation in the one priesthood of Christ.

Although it's certainly true that God has placed anticipations of Christ in the events and people of the Old Testament, it doesn't follow that every event and person in the New Testament is prefigured in the Old. Still, given the centrality of the paschal mystery to holy orders, it's reasonable to expect some prefigurement. Of this, however, the Tradition is silent. This silence may be because such a typological connection does not exist, or perhaps it is because it has yet to be discovered. Finding a type in the Old Testament, grounding it in the Semitic tradition, would go a long way in substantiating the claim of a diaconal priesthood. To identify whether there may be an undiscovered typology of the *mandatum*, we need to identify first what the *mandatum* signifies and whether it was foreshadowed in the Old Testament. In his consideration of the foot-washing, the South African exegete Jan Gabriël Van der Watt observes:

> What was important was not necessarily the action in itself, but rather the character of the action; in other words, the intent and attitude the action illustrates. This might be the reason why there is no known evidence that the practice of foot-washing was continued in the early Church in the sense of the Johannine example. However the requirement of intense love, serving one another, even in humbling tasks, remained part and parcel of Christianity.

If Van der Watt is correct that the intent and attitude of the *mandatum* is intense love, and if we wish to discover a possible typological connection in the Old Testament, we'll need to return to the foot-washing narrative to appreciate the context of that love. This will enable us to fine-tune our search and subsequent examination of any possible typology of a priesthood within the diaconate.

The narrative begins by placing the foot-washing within the Last Supper. John says, "Before the feast of the Passover, when Jesus knew that his hour had come to depart out of this world to the Father, having loved his own who were in the world, he loved them to the end" (Jn 13:1). This reference to loving His disciples "to the end" contextualizes what follows, providing insight into Jesus' motivation, the very reason for this act.

The hour (*hōra*) refers to the climactic event of Jesus' passion, death, and resurrection — this is to say, the very manner in which He will express this love. This direct connection to the paschal mystery means that the intense love expressed in the *mandatum* is of the deepest kind. Of this Jesus says, "Greater love has no man than this, that a man lay down his life for his friends"

(Jn 15:13).

Anticipating His passion through a symbolic expression, Jesus dons the garb of a servant and performs a servant's task — an act unrivaled in antiquity. Here, His intense love is expressed in service, in a redemptive gift of self that wills the good of another for the sake of the other, prefiguring and finding its fulfillment in the cross and resurrection. This is precisely what Jesus meant when He said, "The Son of man came not to be served but to serve, and to give his life as a ransom for many" (Mt 20:28). If the intent and attitude of the *mandatum* is, as Van der Watt observes, intense love, and if that love is expressed in the sacrifice of a servant, then it follows that a possible Old Testament typology will be found in a suffering servant.

In Isaiah 52 and 53, the author describes an enigmatic figure that the Church Fathers would later call the "Suffering Servant." The parallels between this servant who suffers and Jesus are quite striking. Because of this, the early Church wasted little time in making a typological connection between the two. It wasn't so much that the typology rested on two different servants who suffered, but that the suffering they endured was redemptive for others. As Isaiah points out, "he was wounded for our transgressions, / he was bruised for our iniquities … with his stripes we are healed" (Is 53:5).

It's noteworthy that the first recorded biblical figure to recognize Jesus as the Suffering Servant was Philip, one of the first deacons, in his encounter with the Ethiopian eunuch (Acts 8:29–35). This connection is also found in Peter's first epistle (1 Pt 2:22–25). Likewise, the Church Fathers were quick to pick up on this typology. In his *Dialogue with Trypho*, Justin Martyr refers to this text thirty-one times. Indeed, even a superficial survey of patristic literature demonstrates a strong typological connection between the Suffering Servant and Christ. Today, the Church summarizes this identification when she teaches: "By his loving obedience to the Father, 'unto death, even death on a cross' (Phil 2:8), Jesus fulfills the atoning mission (cf. Is 53:10) of the suffering Servant, who will 'make many righteous; and he shall bear their iniquities' (Is 53:11; cf. Rom 5:19)" (CCC 623).

The typological connection between the Suffering Servant and Jesus the Priest, already well established in the Tradition, may seem distinct from a typological connection between the Suffering Servant and Jesus the Servant as expressed in the *mandatum*. This particular typology at first glance may seem tenuous until we shift our focus from the act to the agent, from the foot-washing to the Foot Washer, Jesus Christ.

This shift is key to unlocking this diaconal participation in the one priesthood of Christ. In both examples, we have not two typologies, but one single typology revealed at two different levels. This is to say that the *mandatum*, and the diaconate it institutes, precisely because it is inextricably linked to the paschal mystery, reveals more fully who the Suffering Servant is and why He suffers. It extends an already existing typology rather than revealing a second. Here, the same Suffering Servant referred to prophetically in Isaiah is the one who washed His apostles' feet. Commenting on foot-washing in the Semitic imagination, John Christopher Thomas observes:

> Footwashing is generally the responsibility of servants. While a host/hostess offers hospitable acts, it is ordinarily carried out by his/her slaves, even though the guest may sometimes wash his/her own feet. There is so much identification with servants footwashing that the footbasin comes to function figuratively as a sign of servitude. Those who receive footwashing are always the social superiors of those who render the service.

In many respects, this typology, traditionally thought of as revealing Christ's priesthood, also reveals His servanthood. Indeed, it's precisely in and through His servanthood that His priesthood is exercised. Put another way, Isaiah's Suffering Servant not only reveals Christ's sacrifice (priesthood) but, at the very same time and in the very same respect, reveals His servanthood (diaconate). It also reveals that diaconal ministry, if it's to become what it is, must be priestly at its core.

The deacon, if he grounds his identity in Christ, must see his ministry as sacrificial, as his particular participation in Christ's timeless and eternal sacrifice. It's in this respect that we can properly speak of the priesthood of the diaconate. This priestly quality imbues his diaconate with a redemptive character in which the deacon is capacitated to offer himself in union with Christ through the exercise of his ministry. In this way, like his Master, the deacon acts as both priest and victim. Thus, by "incarnating" Christ the Servant, he also reveals Christ the Priest, albeit in a manner different than the presbyterate. As indicated earlier, this moves his ministry from mere functionality, as holy as these functions may be, to something quite salvific — not only for those he serves, but for himself as well.

Beyond this, the image and typology of the Suffering Servant reveal yet another level of unity between priests and deacons. Where "suffering" represents the priesthood, "servant" represents the diaconate, both of which Christologically interpenetrate one another. As a result, they reveal Christ and His mission in a way that alone they cannot.

Exploring the Implications

Step 1: Personal Reflection
Key Themes:
- The priesthood of the diaconate
- The typology of the Suffering Servant

- The unity of holy orders revealed in the Suffering Servant

Reflection Questions:
- Identify and reflect on two or three things you learned from this chapter that you didn't know before, or now know better, regarding the unity of holy orders.
- Identify and reflect on two or three key spiritual insights you gained from this chapter that will help you in your life and ministry as a priest or deacon.
- Flowing from these insights, identify and reflect on two or three practical ways it might be possible to foster better unity among your brother clerics in your ministerial situation.

Step 2: Communal Sharing
Refer to the "Communal Sharing" section at the end of the introduction on page 44 to complete this step.

CHAPTER 5

RELATIONSHIP, IDENTITY, AND MISSION

In developing the practical implications for greater clerical unity, it would be tempting, given the theological foundations already laid, to jump in and consider the various pragmatic and pastoral elements associated with this approach. To be sure, these practical matters will make up much of this book, but our haste at this point would result in a lack of context and, as they say, context is everything. By context, I mean a simple framework that will help us understand the connection among our relationship to, identity in, and mission with Jesus Christ. Relationship, identity, and mission make up a triad, with their association describing the dynamic proper to any authentic Catholic spirituality and the unity that flows from it.

Several years back, I had the opportunity to make a retreat under the direction of Deacon James Keating. There was only one other retreatant in attendance with me. The retreat was held in

Omaha during one of the summer sessions of the Institute of Priestly Formation (IPF) where Keating was the director of theological formation. A central tenet of IPF is built around the principles of relationship, identity, and mission, known by the acronym RIM. It was developed by IPF's executive director, Fr. Richard Gabuzda, and first delivered in a paper for one of their symposiums. Because RIM is not a static reality but one marked by continuous activity, it will be referred here as the RIM Dynamic.

In its most basic sense, the RIM Dynamic is a simple, three-step, cyclic progression that moves from the interior to the exterior, thereby providing greater integrity between the spiritual and moral life. In doing so, it enables us to become more fully who we are by more fully participating in the grace we've received. During the retreat, Deacon Keating explained RIM and applied it to the diaconate. I was immediately captivated by its simple elegance. It put into words something that had stirred in my heart for many years. I knew that, like the experience of many in priestly formation, much of my diaconal formation lacked a solid spiritual integration. Sure, all seminaries and formation programs address spirituality, but quite often they do so in a rather implied, dispassionate, and external sense, leaving it up to seminarians and diaconal candidates to take it up with their spiritual directors in a more internal way. Though changing for the better in many seminaries, this approach, precisely because it lacks the integration with the other dimensions of formation, is rather inadequate. Moreover, before I can seek unity with another, before I can give myself away, I must first possess myself at least to some degree. This self-possession or maturation, for the Christian, requires by necessity the cultivation of the interior life, such that greater unity with God provides the basis for my unity with others. Consequently, there's a direct and proportionate relationship between my spirituality and my desire to seek unity with other believers. This relationship is analogous to the

Greatest Commandment and a corollary to faith and works and, because of this, it is integral to our particular vocations.

To better grasp the RIM Dynamic (fig. 4a, 4b, 4c), and how it relates to greater unity among the clergy, I'll begin by unpacking each of its three elements. Before doing so, however, it will be necessary to describe how each element — relationship, identity, and mission — interacts with the others so as to better understand its dynamic nature. To accomplish this as it applies to clerical unity, I'll start with two simple examples: unity with God (fig. 4a) followed by marital unity (fig. 4b). Each of these illustrates RIM such that, as we apply it to clerical unity (fig. 4c), a foundation has been laid. This, in turn, will provide a fuller ap-

Three Examples of the RIM Dynamic

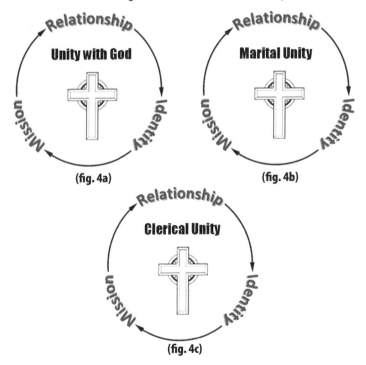

(fig. 4a)

(fig. 4b)

(fig. 4c)

preciation of RIM and its implications for greater unity among bishops, priests, and deacons.

Unity with God

Unity with God begins through a cultivation of the interior life, which is a response to grace. This grace can be described as God calling each one of us personally to himself, subtly at first, and growing in intensity over time. As we pursue the God who pursues us, a relationship is formed and, if this relationship is actively engaged, it matures. At some point in time, this relationship imparts an identity to the one who pursues it. In the case of the priest or deacon, this occurs at ordination. His relationship with God, at this point, becomes so intense that, at the core of his being, he becomes priest or deacon. The more he actively engages in this relationship, the more he grasps the profound implications of his new identity in Christ. With this identity in place, and by virtue of the sacred powers associated with the order received, his identity now gives rise to mission. Mission, as applied to individual bishops, priests, and deacons, is expressed in their life and ministry. Thus, in the very exercise of their particular ministry, they express and bear witness not simply to their relationship to God, but to their identity in Him and their mission with Him. In this respect, they "incarnate" that same God, in a more integral sense, who is both priest and deacon.

This process is not linear but cyclic. This is to say that as his mission is exercised, his relationship is matured, his identity is intensified, and his mission is made more effective. This movement, in turn, reveals RIM as a dynamic, not only as a progression between each of its three elements in a given cycle, but as one cycle gives way to another and another and another. Within and around each cycle, the priest or deacon grows in more intimate communion with God and, in doing so, grows in holiness. This is precisely why the interior life is so essential to clerical unity, for it is here we encounter God most intimately.

Marital Unity

Where the above example describes RIM on a personal level, it can also be extended communally (see fig. 4b). As applied to marital unity, this begins with the attraction to another, which extends beyond mere infatuation. At first, the one being attracted perceives something special in the other — something unique that gives rise to the desire for greater unity. If this attraction is mutual, courtship begins, at which time the mystery of the other is revealed and a relationship is formed. When this relationship is actively engaged by both parties, it matures over time. At some point, this relationship imparts a new identity to the couple. This occurs at marriage or, more specifically, at the exchange of vows. Here, their relationship becomes so intense that he becomes husband and she becomes wife. The more they actively engage in this relationship, the more they grasp the profound implications of their new identity in Christ. With this identity in place, and by virtue of the grace associated with holy matrimony, this new identity now gives rise to mission. Thus, in the very living out of their marriage, they express and bear witness not simply to their identity as a married couple but to their relationship to God, "incarnating" Him in their shared life and children.

As in the case with our earlier example, this process is not linear but cyclic. As their mission is exercised, their relationship is matured, their identity as husband and wife is intensified, and their mission is made more effective. Once again, this movement reveals RIM as a dynamic, not only as a progression between each of its three elements in a given cycle, but as one cycle gives way to another and another and another. Within and around each cycle, the couple grows in greater intimate communion with one another and with God. As a direct consequence, they also grow in holiness, orienting them to their final end in Christ Jesus.

Clerical Unity

The above two examples demonstrate the RIM Dynamic both personally, as in union with God, and communally, as in marriage. With these established, a strong foundation is now laid to explore the application of RIM as it relates to clerical unity. In the above diagram (fig. 4c), the inner part of the circle represents the desired goal: intimate communion with Christ Jesus, who is both deacon and priest. Indeed, it's only in and through our concrete pursuit of unity with one another that this ultimate goal is slowly realized for, as Jesus reminds us, "As you did it to one of the least of these my brethren, you did it to me" (Mt 25:40). Greater union with God isn't possible outside of greater union with one another.

As we've already seen in the Establishment Hypothesis, this union is most fully expressed in the paschal mystery from which arise the origins of holy orders as it relates to the mission of the Church. The desire for greater intimate communion with Christ thus provides the fundamental starting point for RIM and roots that unity in a divine love outpoured. This unity bespeaks a state of oneness where all believers are gathered in Christ. If this union is pursued, it's always in a state of becoming, uniting us cohesively with Him and with every other believer through baptism, such that we make up the one Body of Christ (see Eph 5:30; 1 Cor 12:12–21).

Relationship to Christ

This unity has a particular application to the clergy, who should personify it in their relationships with one another, relationships that should inspire and embolden the laity to a similar oneness proper to their own vocation. Absent this fundamental truth and its practical implications, clerical unity is an ideological construct that exists only in the abstract as an unobtainable ideal. Though noble in itself, such a purely speculative approach insulates itself from individual responsibility, out of which flows Jesus' prayer to the Father, "that they may all be one; even as you, Father, are in me, and I in you, that they also may be in us, so that the world may believe that you have sent me" (Jn 17:21). Notice how, in Jesus' prayer, a prayer contextualized within the invitation to love one another (Jn 13:34), unity is central to belief in Him. This belief, in turn, is crucial to the mystery of salvation and the mission of the Church. Thus, if we are to fulfill our vocations, unity can't be trivialized or merely tolerated but must be personally appropriated and actively sought.

Unity presupposes, as its fundamental basis, an interpersonal relationship. It bespeaks our connectedness with and to one another. To the extent that this connectedness grows, unity grows with it. In this respect, unity isn't so much the end sought, but instead is the consequence of an ongoing healthy relationship, which at its core involves the willingness of both parties to share something of their lives with one another. Regardless of the kind of relationship, it's marked by an ongoing willingness to gift oneself to another, grounded in a mutual love of Christ, such that it's a particular participation in divine love. Christ then, as we've already seen, is the source of this sharing and the foundation of the relationship between bishops, priests, and deacons.

Like His own gift of self, revealed most fully in the paschal mystery, Christ calls bishops, priests, and deacons to gift themselves to one another for the good of the other and for the sake of the Church. This call imposes a moral obligation on the one accepting it. In this regard, it's freely self-imposed in that it's a natural consequence of responding to Christ. We now, as a result of this response, take on a new personal responsibility to grow in greater unity with one another as part and parcel of growing in greater intimate communion with God. As attested to multiple times throughout Scripture and Tradition, unity with God and unity with others are inextricably linked, such that they are meaningless apart from one another. It's precisely through loving others that we love God, and it's precisely through loving God that we're capable of loving one another.

In order to give of himself, one must first possess himself sufficiently, for without this self-possession, there's nothing to give. Simply put, we cannot give what we don't first possess. This self-possession has both subjective and objective dimensions. Whereas the subjective dimension involves the spiritual, psychological, and emotional maturity of the cleric to give himself and receive others, the objective involves an ever-deepening grasp of what it means to be who he is as a cleric. Consequently, if a bishop, priest, or deacon has an impoverished appreciation of what it means to be a bishop, priest, or deacon as the Church understands it, then his ability to create, foster, and grow clerical relationships will be diminished and, with it, the unity that flows.

This understanding extends not simply to the cleric's own sense of ecclesial identity, but how he grasps the identity of those in the holy orders he shares. Put another way, the ability to share oneself is dependent upon the sharer's understanding of the one to whom he shares, such that his manner of sharing corresponds to the other rendering his sharing intelligible and acceptable. Indeed, just as verbal communication requires that we use the language of the one with whom we're communicating, so too the one who shares must possess a basic understanding of the ecclesial identity of the one to whom he shares himself. This ecclesial identity, if it's to be authentic, must be grounded in the Church's own understanding, and therefore the cleric ought to seek to constantly refine his own understanding to the mind and heart of the Church. Therefore, if a bishop, priest, or deacon has an impoverished appreciation of the other as a bishop, priest, or deacon, then his ability to create, foster, and grow clerical relationships will be diminished and, with it, the unity that flows.

Unlike the priesthood which, over the centuries, developed a robust theology, the diaconate had but a rudimentary and fragmented theology when it was restored by the Second Vatican Council. Without a clear sense of what the diaconate is, and its unique contribution to the mystery of salvation, it's difficult to develop an authentic diaconal theology. Indeed, without this understanding, the deacon's sense of ecclesial self is diminished, along with his ability to unite with others more effectively in ministry. Similarly, if a bishop or priest also possesses an impoverished understanding of his own diaconate as it relates to being a bishop or priest, then his ability to share himself with the diaconate is equally diminished, and his pastoral ministry rendered less effective.

Herein lies one of the main obstacles to clerical unity. As noted earlier, little attention is paid to the theology of the diaconate during priestly formation, and scarcely more is paid during diaconal formation. None if any of the recent developments made on the theology of the diaconate have made their way into the mainstream of clerical formation, be it priestly or diaconal. Since all bishops are drawn from the priesthood, and since the priesthood has an impoverished understanding of the diaconate by virtue of its formation or lack thereof, then it follows that bishops, unless they make a personal effort, possess this same poverty. Moreover, if what we said earlier about all priests being deacons is true, and it is, then it follows that this lack of diaconal theology is not a problem confined to the diaconate alone, but is shared by all clergy and, to a lesser extent, the laity.

To sum things up, relationship stands as the fundamental starting point for the RIM Dynamic. It is, in many respects, a twofold relationship, first having to do with love of God, and then, from this, love of neighbor (in this application, other members of the clergy). Though we can distinguish between these relationships, we can never separate them, as they're really two parts of the same whole, interpenetrating one another. Where love of God gives purpose and meaning to love of neighbor, love of neighbor enables us to respond to God's love in concrete and practical ways. It allows the love of God to move from our interior to our exterior, enabling us to "incarnate" Him in our life and ministry. With this now established, we can turn to what arises from all interpersonal relationships: identity. This represents the second part of the RIM triad and one that has deep personal implications.

Identity in Christ

As we've already seen, all relationships, to a greater or lesser extent, give rise to a deeper sense of identity. It's important to recognize that this new identity doesn't represent something other than who we are. We don't become someone else, adopting foreign traits and strange ways. Rather, if the relationship is healthy, this new identity strengthens and fulfills who we already know ourselves to be. In many respects, we become more fully who we are, more fully alive. Put another way, the bishop becomes more a bishop, the priest more a priest, and the deacon more a deacon. This is simply an application of grace perfecting nature.

The sanctifying grace received at the reception of the sacraments comes about through an intense encounter that configures us to Christ. This grace capacitates us to rise above the effects of sin, enabling us to become what God fully intends us to be, revealing who we really are. Applied here, the sanctifying grace associated with holy orders enables the cleric to live out his identity, realizing his final end, intimate communion with the Trinity, forever. It gives him a sense of who he really is. In this respect, he so identifies with Christ that, in a certain sense, he more effectively becomes the Christ he was configured to be. This is accomplished in the exercise of his ministry, which is his particular contribution to the mission of the Church.

Mission with Christ

Pope St. John Paul II was fond of remarking that the Church doesn't have a mission, she *is* a mission. In his 1990 encyclical *Redemptoris Missio*, he writes, "This definitive self-revelation of God is the fundamental reason why the Church is missionary by her very nature. She cannot do other than proclaim the Gospel." Later, Pope Francis would become more specific about the manner in which he sees this mission exercised. In *Evangelii Gaudium*, he writes:

> I prefer a Church which is bruised, hurting and dirty because it has been out on the streets, rather than a Church which is unhealthy from being confined and from clinging to its own security. … More than by fear of going astray, my hope is that we will be moved by the fear of remaining shut up within structures which give us a false sense of security, within rules which make us harsh judges, within habits which make us feel safe, while at our door people are starving. (49)

Understood this way, mission stands at the very heart of the Church. It's her reason for being, her sole focus, and, because of this, her highest work. This work, though singular in purpose, admits of a diversity of expression. Thus John Paul II writes, "Mission is a single but complex reality, and it develops in a variety of ways."

Although all of the faithful belong to this mission, the clergy are called to live it out in a specific way, sharing in Christ's own mission of salvation in a way that supports and complements the mission of the laity, who are equally called, albeit in different ways. Properly understood, the ministry of the bishop, priest, and deacon always takes place within the broader mission of the Church. It's a specific participation in, and a realization of, the call to go and make disciples of all nations (Mt 28:19). Although there are many ways to exercise this call, all require service as a fundamental and indispensable component.

Thus service, as described earlier, stands as the essential means by which the Church carries out her mission. Without service, without *diakonia*, the Church cannot fulfill her mandate, and Christ's passion, death, and resurrection are emptied of their saving power, relegating the Good News to a noble but abstract and unattainable concept. Consequently, it's precisely in and through service, the living out of the cleric's relationship to and identity in Christ, that mission becomes tangible and salvation attainable. The life and ministry of the cleric, when it's intentionally lived out in faith, allows Christ's mission to be realized and personalized such that we hear with His ears, see with His eyes, and touch with His hands. Indeed, just as the Incarnation was essential to Our Lord's ministry, so, too, each in our own way, the cleric's own "incarnation" is necessary to continue that ministry under the guidance of the Holy Spirit.

Ministry is the concrete living out of the Church's mission. It's the cleric's particular contribution, expressed through his particular vocation and realized in a particular way through his personality. This unique contribution renders Christ's mission real, grounding itself in the very here-and-now and enmeshing itself in the very fabric of our lives. In this respect, the Church, in order to fulfill her God-given mission, can rightly be called a Servant Church, precisely because she is directed toward the integral human good. As Pope Benedict observed in his 2005 encyclical, *Deus Caritas Est*, "The Church's deepest nature is expressed in her three-fold responsibility: of proclaiming the word of God (*kerygma-martyria*), celebrating the sacraments (*leitourg-ia*), and exercising the ministry of charity (*diakonia*). These duties presuppose each other and are inseparable" (25).

This is why the diaconate of bishops, priests, and deacons is so essential to the mission of the Church, and why their unity and witness to Christ the Servant are so crucial to the mystery of salvation. This also illustrates why this common diaconate among all clergy and its witness provides a means to greater unity, as that unity is realized in the mission of the Church. Of this Pope St. John Paul II writes, "Without witnesses there can be no witness, just as without missionaries there can be no missionary activity."

The mission of the Church, conveyed in her missionary activity, is realized in our witness to Christ, which finds, for the cleric, its concrete expression in ministerial service, be it episcopal, presbyteral, or diaconal. The call for clerics to bear witness to Christ the Servant is a call to bear witness to the One who exercised the greatest act of service through His redemptive sacrifice on the cross. It's to see in that service, and in the mission it seeks to fulfill, its real meaning: a redemptive love outpoured.

In many respects, the paschal mystery is the measure by which all service, all acts of love, are measured. Because it brought about salvation, it stands at the very foundation of the Church's saving mission. This is precisely because it refines our understanding of service as an interpersonal reality, as a salvific gift of self that wills the good of the other for the sake of the other. In doing so, it can accommodate and integrate personal suffering as a sanctifying element, elevating and transforming service to a love that is sacrificial in nature. This is nothing less than a participation in the redemptive suffering of Christ, giving our service the quality of a divine love. Service, understood this way, gives love its outward expression and, in this regard, advances the Church's mission. It makes love "transferable," so to speak, through concrete acts that reach beyond ourselves to the hearts of those we serve. As St. Augustine of Hippo so beautifully observes, "What does love look like? It has the hands to help others. It has the feet to hasten to the poor and needy. It has eyes to see misery and want. It has the ears to hear the sighs and sorrows of men. That is what love looks like."

This is not at all to suggest that human love can compare to, or replace, divine love. Rather, it's to assert that when human love, human service, is infused with divine love, it becomes far more than it is. In this regard, mission is not effective without an ever-deepening sense of identity, precisely because this sense of identity, grounded in an ever-deepening relationship with Jesus Christ, gives rise to mission. Mission, then, is a natural consequence of identity, which itself is a natural consequence of relationship. In many respects, this is the essence of RIM and why it's so essential to the Church's mission. It not only illustrates the dynamic between our interior and exterior lives, but it integrates and facilitates them as well, rendering our ministry, and the role it plays in the Church's mission, far more effective.

Putting It All Together

Mission, as an act of divine love expressed in clerical unity, completes the RIM circle and, at the very same time, begins it anew. This is because, in the very carrying out of our mission, we grow in intimate communion with the Christ we serve. This enriches our relationship with Him, which in turn deepens our identity, rendering our mission even more effective. Thus, as we've already seen, far from being a static once-around-the-circle reality, RIM is a dynamic that can continue throughout the life of clerics. By integrating the interior and exterior aspects of our lives, it enables us to continually discover, in the here-and-now, our unique role in the life of the Church.

Having considered RIM on a personal level, we can now

turn our attention to its cumulative effects as these effects relate to each grade of holy orders and the mission of the Church.
The underlying assumption here is that each order — bishop,
priest, and deacon — contributes something the others do not,
and that these contributions, along with that of the laity, reflect
something of the *Christus Totus*. In this respect, although there
remains a hierarchy within holy orders, among the grades there
exists a necessary complementarity. This complementarity is illustrated in the diagram below (fig. 5). Note that each grade of
holy orders makes its own particular contribution, and that this
contribution is realized and expressed in the RIM Dynamic. As
these come together under the local bishop, they advance the

The Application of RIM to the Unity of Holy Orders and the Mission of the Church (fig. 5)

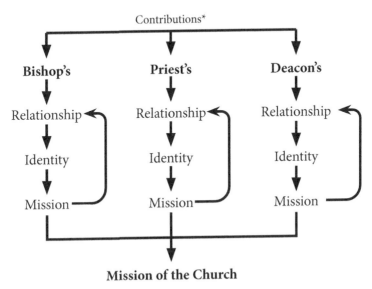

*Religious and laity are omitted for the sake of clarity and focus.

mission of the broader Church as that mission is carried out in the local church. This is because the very "engine" that drives each order within RIM — divine love — now drives, in and through these orders, the mission of the Church.

As we conclude our consideration of RIM, it's important to recognize that, when applied personally and cumulatively, the dynamic provides a corrective to what can best be called *the rush to mission*. This rush arises out of a culture that places too much emphasis on functionality and too little on relationships, often reducing human beings to human doings. If, for instance, a pastor wants more extraordinary ministers of the Eucharist for Mass, we typically put an announcement in the bulletin, have a night or two of training on the functionality of dispensing our Eucharistic Lord, and then assign ministers to various Masses. In most cases, little to no thought is given to the lay minister's relationship with or identity to Christ, often rendering their ministry void of the very transformative power it possesses. Indeed, in its extreme, this way of formation serves not to draw them to greater intimacy with the One who calls them to minister but instead allows them to hide behind what they do. As a result, the doing of the ministry itself becomes the primary way of relating to Christ, such that the spiritual element is reduced to mere function.

By reducing ministry to the thing being done, ministers don't have to render themselves vulnerable; they don't have to open up to Christ. All they have to do is punch their "piety ticket" by doing the ministry and then go home. This is not to undermine the essential value of lay service as a participation in the mission of the Church, but to assert that, without relationship and identity, the value of that mission, that service, remains superficial. God does not want our doing. He wants our being, and if we surrender our being to Him (relationship), He elevates and transforms us (identity) and, because of this, infuses our ministry with divine love (mission). As the psalmist says, "For you take no delight in sacrifice; / were I to give a burnt offering, you would not be pleased. / The sacrifice acceptable to God is a broken spirit; / a broken and contrite heart, O God, you will not despise" (Ps 51:16–17). At the risk of being redundant, ministry then, as a participation in the mission of the Church, is the result of something more profound: relationship and identity. Consequently, without these two prior elements, mission is undermined and with it the very Gospel it seeks to proclaim.

Grounding RIM in the Establishment Hypothesis

Thus far, in our consideration of RIM, we've used a more rational approach to describe the association between relationship, identity, and mission as it relates to clerical unity. Although on one level this is certainly sufficient to illustrate the dynamic's value, a closer examination reveals another, more profound level — one that corresponds to Divine Revelation, grounding RIM in God's own self-disclosure and His plan for our salvation.

As you may have already noticed, in working out some of the challenges associated with pushing the theological and philosophical envelope on clerical unity, I use diagrams. Although these diagrams don't exhaust the mystery being pondered, they act as graphic clues, pointing beyond themselves to deeper realities. They also allow me a way to better understand and articulate the concept under consideration, "packaging" it so to speak, in a way that can be shared. Often, I'll post these illustrations on the bulletin board in my office so I can continue to contemplate and refine them. I had already posted the Establishment Hypothesis as shown earlier in figure 2. It struck me that, whereas this lineal diagram eventually becomes circular, beginning and ending with Christ, perhaps it would be interesting to draw it that way. This would better illustrate the dynamic quality of the hypothesis along with Jesus, the Alpha and Omega (Rv

1:8; 21:6; 22:13), as its source. This circular expression, crudely drawn, was placed on my bulletin board next to the illustration of the RIM Dynamic (fig. 4a). Each time I entered my office, something struck me about these two drawings beyond their common geometry. I began to see, over time, that the two illustrations were not two separate and distinct realities only casually related, but two interrelated aspects of a single reality.

Pondering how this could be, I was moved to superimpose the RIM illustration around the Establishment Hypothesis as two independent concentric circles (fig. 6). In what best can be

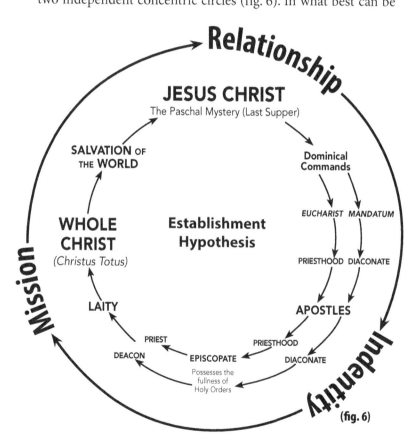

(fig. 6)

described as an "Aha!" moment, I was able to see how RIM is not merely a sound, rational approach to clerical unity, but how the hypothesis grounds RIM in Divine Revelation. This was jaw-dropping to me and something I never expected to find. Immediately, I began to see three sets of correlations corresponding to relationship, identity, and mission. The first and most obvious of these is that relationship correlated with Jesus Christ and the paschal mystery. His redemptive act reconciled us with the Father and brought about a new relationship with God, which was opened to His apostles and through them to the whole of humanity to constitute the Church. The second and equally obvious correlation is that, just as relationship gives rise to identity, in the Establishment Hypothesis, the paschal mystery gives rise to the episcopate, presbyterate, and diaconate. Here, the identity of the cleric, grounded in an ontological change, flows from his relationship to Christ as expressed in His passion, death, resurrection, and ascension. Depending on the order received, he is bishop, he is priest, he is deacon. From this, the third and final correlation is the natural consequence of the first two. Just as identity gives rise to mission, so too bishops, priests, and deacons, by virtue of their configuration to Christ, now share in His mission proper to their order (Jn 19:21).

All of this suggests that the same "engine" that drives the hypothesis drives RIM, a salvific gift of self that wills the good of the other for the sake of the other. It's nothing less than an intimate participation in the redemptive love of God, calling all, saints and sinners alike, to His bosom. In doing so, it reveals a final and deeply profound insight — that of the very Trinity itself.

As one God in three Divine Persons, they're not just one relationship among relationships, but the source and measure of all other relationships. Within the Trinity, this relationship gives rise to identity as Father, Son, and Holy Spirit. This Trinitarian identity, in turn, gives rise to mission as expressed first in creation and then, after the Fall, redemption as part of the divine plan from the beginning. All of this means that, by internalizing and applying the Establishment Hypothesis and RIM to our lives, clerical unity becomes a natural consequence. It finds its ultimate source and meaning as an intimate participation in the love of the Trinity. This is why clerical unity can't be secondary to the cleric but is essential to his relationship to, identity in, and mission with Christ, as that Christ is revealed in his brother clerics.

Developing a Unity Plan

Any attempt to use this book to achieve greater clerical unity won't succeed if it's not continued beyond its individual reading. What is presented in these pages is a recommended "springboard" to this unity, a launching point, whose sustainability will depend on the willingness of its members to cooperate with grace and commit, long-term, to that very same grace. Jesus, the Messiah, is the great gathering force, a force grounded in the paschal mystery and extended to each of us as an invitation to love one another. By establishing His kingdom on earth, Jesus displaces the prince of this world. Whereas Jesus gathers us in love, inviting us to deeper communion, Satan and his minions undermine that communion by enticing us to sin. This typically begins with subtle thoughts that meeting together as clergy is a waste of time and counterproductive to an already busy schedule. It can take the form of personal dislike for members of the group exacerbated by our own pride and vanity. Consequently, if the effort toward greater unity ends with this book, then we've succumbed to the temptations of the Evil One. This is why, upon its completion and to the extent possible, a plan needs to be developed to continue it in some form.

It's beyond the scope of this or any book to provide a universal detailed plan to foster ongoing unity within the group. This level of specificity requires an understanding of each member, along with the pastoral situation in which he finds himself. What will be presented, as we conclude, are some of the universal factors for sustaining a unity effort as these relate to building a local plan. As with the process recommended in this book, these are only suggestions to spur greater discussion. They are in no way meant to box the group in — only to provide sound guidance.

This will require some work on the front end, particularly as certain structures and programs are developed to move forward. As a result, it's not sufficient simply to schedule regular meetings and let the Holy Spirit work out the agenda. This form of providentialism, although it might sound good and noble, will ultimately fail because the Holy Spirit doesn't reward the lazy. For authentic and lasting unity to be achieved, the Spirit must permeate and penetrate the entire process, including the tough work on the front end. The following are some practical recommendations for developing a unity plan within the group.

Establishing the Group: As noted earlier, the group should consist of those who've either worked through this book together or who come later and are willing to read it. It should consist exclusively of clergy, as this defines the kind of unity sought. Though it can be used to foster unity within the grades of holy orders, its best use is that among the grades, highlighting the unity of the sacrament. The group should center around a particular ministerial activity, such as a common parish assignment. In large parishes, this could consist of all the priests or deacons. In smaller parishes with limited clergy, this may consist of priests and deacons who gather from a number of neighboring parishes. Though group size is a factor in the ability to share effectively, in large groups exceeding eight, this can be mitigated by breakout sessions and then coming together to share key observations and insights at the end.

Group Facilitator: To ensure continuity and consistency, the group will need a regular facilitator. Because this is typically a parish gathering, it should be led by a pastor who is highly motivated, organized, and willing to sustain the vision of unity among the members. Absent this, the pastor may designate another member, be it a priest or deacon, to facilitate the group.

The facilitator is a member who helps the group to collaborate better, understand their common objectives, and plan how to achieve these objectives. He must listen well, be open to suggestions and, when there is not unanimity, put things to a vote. It's also his primary responsibility to keep the sessions on schedule, respecting the members' time and ensuring that all have the opportunity to share to the extent they wish. In many respects, he's the single most important factor in maintaining the cohesiveness of the group and achieving its end. If it's the desire of the pastor and beneficial to the group, the facilitator may be rotated among the members, though this should be after a suitable period, perhaps a year or so. If the facilitator is respected and effective, then he should stay in place unless intervening personal and pastoral factors make it too difficult.

Group Members: As discussed earlier, the members are drawn exclusively from all three grades where possible. Though in a perfect world, all should be motivated to seek unity and see value in this process, there will be some who are highly motivated, others who are generally open, and still others who are not. All potential members of the group should be extended an open invitation to at least the initial six sessions corresponding to the introduction and the five chapters of this book. This may be made mandatory by the pastor as part of ongoing formation, with subsequent sessions being voluntary. Commitment to actively participate by each member ensures the integrity of the group, though this should be implicit and not take a public form. In all cases, the freedom of the members to continue beyond any mandatory ongoing formation — if it is implemented — should be respected by all members of the group. Although there will be a natural hierarchy in the group, all members of the group should be given equal respect and voice.

Meeting Places, Days, and Times: To prevent confusion, a particular meeting place should be selected and used on a regular basis. It should be comfortable, and the members should face each other in a setting that most closely resembles a living room and not a conference room. If, as in the case with combined parishes, there's a desire to rotate meeting places, then it's recommended that this be done over period of time and not every other meeting. So, for instance, the group might meet at one parish for six months and then shift to the other for another six months. A particular day should be sought that suits all or at least the majority of members. Consistency here is also helpful. Likewise, a regular time should be selected as well. Depending on the schedules of the priests and deacons, this might best happen in the afternoons or evenings, as it's less likely that a funeral or other unscheduled pastoral activity may interrupt.

Frequency of Meetings: The meetings should be scheduled close enough together so as to provide continuity, and far enough apart so as to give members time to read, meditate, and reflect. Although the precise frequency will be determined by the group, varying with personal and pastoral considerations, it is recommended that they are spaced no less than two weeks apart and no more than a month apart. This interval should be set and a schedule made in advance so that every member can adequately prepare and more fully participate.

Content of Meetings: Initially, the content under discussion will consist of this book, with the initial six meetings corresponding to the introduction and five chapters. At the fourth meeting, members should be thinking about how they want to proceed after the original six meetings. By the fifth meeting, they should discuss these possibilities so that at the sixth and final meeting they can schedule the next series of meetings based on new content. The content can either be something developed by the group itself or existing materials already available. This can take the form of a Bible study, spiritual enrichment, book review, or some other packaged religious program. It should follow the process as recommended in ongoing formation by integrating, to a greater or lesser degree, all four dimensions: intellectual, human, spiritual, and pastoral. The content and its reasonable breakdown will determine the number of sessions in the series. Should the discussion prove fruitful, and should the group not finish the chapter before the scheduled end of the session, it may be continued in the next session. Here, the most important thing is the sharing as it relates to greater unity.

Commitment to Pray for One Another: Although this section has provided some practical steps on forming and maintaining the group, all of these require grace if they're to be sustained and if they're to achieve the goal of greater unity. One way to help ensure this desired end is to commit to some level of prayer each day for each member of the group. Although individual members should decide how this will be integrated into their own prayer lives, its purpose is to avail ourselves of the grace so essential for unity in Christ and to bond the group in the power of the Holy Spirit. In this regard, the group may wish to put themselves under the patronage of the Blessed Virgin Mary or perhaps the patron saint of the parish. The grace flowing from this daily prayer will also have the effect of reminding us of and sensitizing us to the truth that unity must also occur apart from the sessions as well as inside. It helps extend the sessions beyond themselves to other aspects of our interaction, allowing the transformative grace of God's unifying love to be expressed in our actions.

Exploring the Implications

Step 1: Personal Reflection
Key Themes:
- The RIM Dynamic
- Integrating RIM in clerical unity
- Developing a unity plan

Reflection Questions:
- Identify and reflect on two or three things you learned from this chapter that you didn't know before, or now know better, regarding the unity of holy orders.
- Identify and reflect on two or three key spiritual insights you gained from this chapter that will help you in your life and ministry as a priest or deacon.
- Flowing from these insights, identify and reflect on two or three practical ways it might be possible to foster better unity among your brother clerics in your ministerial situation.

Step 2: Communal Sharing
Refer to the "Communal Sharing" section at the end of the introduction on page 44 to complete this step.

CONCLUSION

I began this book with the observation that the Church of the future lies in the present. From this statement, I posed the question: What will the Church, on the parish level, look like ten, twenty, or even a hundred years from now? More to the point, what can we do as bishops, priests, and deacons to effect a change for the better and advance the sacred mission with which we've been entrusted? It's within this context that I further observed that, although we can't know the future with certainty, we can nevertheless advance the mission of the Church tomorrow through greater clerical unity today.

Although I've provided a theological grounding for this unity, it's treated in this book as a kind of first principle. By this I mean that I see clerical unity as a fundamental, foundational, and self-evident proposition that serves as the starting point for anticipating the future of the Church. In this respect, it plays a crucial role in providing a solid basis for preparing us today for the uncertainties of tomorrow.

The primary challenge this book has attempted to address

is that of clerical disunity. The causes of this discord are many and varied and, although worth exploring, are better left for another time. This is not, in any way, to undermine the value of this exploration. Instead, it's to assert that whatever they are, in whatever form they manifest, the various remedies share one fundamental cure: unity in Christ Jesus.

In this respect, the unity of holy orders is not a unity found in something, in simply the sharing of a sacrament, but in the sharing of Someone. It's precisely because He is indivisibly the *sacerdos* and *diakonos*, and precisely because He is our beginning and end, our all in all, that we turn to Him. If we wish to avoid living a Christological dualism, if we wish to draw into a deeper, more intimate communion with the One who loved us while we were yet sinners, the work of unity is not an option but a privilege that comes to us in the form of a divine invitation. Unity among the clergy is, in its essence, unity with Christ. Any attempt to seek Our Lord without the work of clerical unity is to pass right by Him.

Characterizing this unity as an arduous work is to identify it for what it is. It is and will be laborious; however, it's a labor that, although challenging and demanding, brings about a profound sense of accomplishment and satisfaction. Though this will require significant effort, overcoming obstacles, dying to self, and dedicating ourselves with perseverance, it is, nonetheless, a labor aided by divine help. This is because clerical unity lies in the very heart of Christ. It's His will. As a direct result, the satisfaction derived from this type of labor goes beyond mere completion of the tasks. It's about journeying with one another in Christ. This provides the motivation and grace necessary to undergo what, at times, will be an arduous effort fraught with a thousand and one reasons to quit. This temptation, which arises out of our own concupiscence and is exacerbated by demonic forces, must be resisted. Just as there is no resurrection without the cross, so there is no unity without work, often hard work, often thankless work, but always good work.

In turning to the very source of our vocation, let us never forget that, at the foot of the cross and indeed, the foot of our own crosses, is the company of the Blessed Virgin Mary. Just as she comforted and gave strength to her Son simply by her presence, so too does she extend that same comfort, that same strength, to her sons in the clergy in their joint mission to proclaim the redemptive love of Christ by living out fully our vocations. As Mother of the Church, she is also mother of priests and deacons precisely because she is the mother of *the* Priest, *the* Deacon, her Son. Beyond this singular role, she is a preeminent model of the priesthood by virtue of her sacrifice and, at the same time, she is the preeminent model of the diaconate by virtue of her service.

Let us never fail to turn to her in breaking down the obstacles to clerical unity so that, in all things, Christ is glorified, the Gospel is proclaimed, and salvation is offered.

Mary, Mother of the Clergy, pray for us.

APPENDIX

SPIRITUAL DIRECTION FOR DEACONS

In order to effectively fulfill the Church's mission within the context of their lives and ministries, bishops, priests, and deacons need to constantly cultivate the interior life. Beyond the pious reception of the sacraments and immersing themselves in the word of God, this cultivation requires ongoing spiritual direction. Although the *National Directory for the Formation, Ministry, and Life of Permanent Deacons in the United States* does require that aspirants and candidates have priests as spiritual directors, it does not make that same requirement for deacons. This strikes me as rather odd. Although there are many excellent lay spiritual directors, why is it that priests are only required for aspirants and candidates and not for deacons themselves? On this, the *Directory* is silent.

The value of having a priest as a spiritual director, beyond the availability of reconciliation, is that he too is a deacon and, because he is a deacon, he can identify with his directee in a way that a lay person cannot. Consequently, it follows that if aspirants and candidates require a priest, would not a deacon require one as well?

The answer to this question may be more pragmatic than theological, as there are few priests who offer spiritual direction and those few, it's thought, might be better used for aspirants and candidates. However, even here, it's the universal experience that directors of formation are hard pressed to find priest spiritual directors among the presbyterate, even for those in formation.

So that more priests and deacons may consider entering into the ministry of spiritual direction for aspirants, candidates, and deacons, I've incorporated into this book a small text published by the Diocese of Phoenix entitled *A Guide for the Spiritual Direction of Permanent Deacons*. This excellent publication was included with the approval of Bishop John P. Dolan of Phoenix. It's a concise, easy-to-read guide designed to help those spiritual directors or those discerning this ministry to more effectively direct their directees. The guide is also useful to aspirants, candidates, and deacons to better understand the nature of spiritual direction and to more fully enter into its grace. Individual copies are available through the Diocese of Phoenix Diaconate Office.

I'm very grateful to Bishop Dolan and to the Diocese of Phoenix for allowing the integration of their guide into this book. I pray that it inspires more priests and deacons to take up the spiritual direction of deacons.

A Guide to Directing Permanent Deacons
Overview of Guide

The purpose of this guide is to provide some assistance to those providing spiritual direction to permanent deacons and men in formation for the permanent diaconate. According to the *National Directory*, deacons are called to live a life of mature Christian spirituality "to attain an interior spiritual maturity requires an intense sacramental and prayer life."

Spiritual direction is an essential element in helping deacons to focus on their spiritual lives and to grow into this interior spiritual maturity. This guide also provides encouragement and guidance to the deacons and men in formation as they respond to this call to spiritual maturity.

While not intending to be a comprehensive resource on the subject of spiritual direction, this guide covers the following areas: the contemplative approach to spiritual direction, the relationship between spiritual direction and the Sacrament of Penance, the relationship between spiritual direction and pastoral counseling, guidelines for the first spiritual direction session, and some information pertaining to the state of life of the permanent deacon that may be helpful for the spiritual director.

Spiritual direction is "directly concerned with a person's actual experiences of the relationship with God." Spiritual direction can be defined as assistance given by the director that helps the directee to "pay attention to God's personal communication to him … to respond to this personally communicating God, to grow in intimacy with this God, and to live out the consequences of the relationship."

Just as there are many schools of spirituality within the Catholic Church, there are also many possible approaches to spiritual direction. Given the fact that other approaches are possible, it is nonetheless recommended that a contemplative approach be taken. With such an approach, the spiritual director is primarily concerned with helping to foster the directee's personal relationship with God. The spiritual director seeks to be in a contemplative posture of listening to both God and the directee, and as he is listening, he is helping the directee to notice and to "stay with" the movements of God in his own heart. Nonetheless, there are times when the director, responding to the promptings of the Holy Spirit, needs to "ask questions, to give information, or express opinion." Ultimately it will be up to the priest-director to discern the best approach, though always cognizant of the fact that spiritual direction is "the guiding of a person into a life truly under the dominion of the Holy Spirit, who is the primary director."

A Contemplative Approach to Spiritual Direction

As mentioned in the introduction, it is recommended that a "contemplative approach" to spiritual direction be taken. In a contemplative approach, the primary relationship is between God and the directee. The spiritual director simply facilitates the growth of this primary relationship. The spiritual director seeks to remain deeply rooted in his own place of interior intimacy with God so that he is able to have "one ear" attuned to God and his "other ear" attuned to the directee. In this way the spiritual director is able to "get out of the way" and serve as a pure instrument of God.

The relationships involved might be best illustrated with the following diagram:

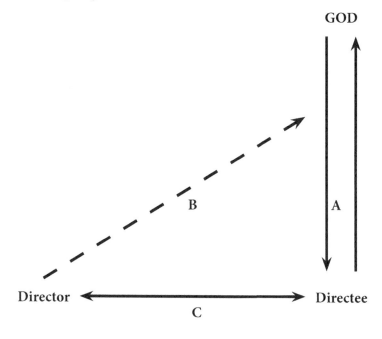

In the above diagram, the primary relationship is A: The conversation between God and the directee. God is communicating personally to the directee and the directee is responding to God. Line B illustrates that what the spiritual director is primarily attentive to is this conversation between God and the directee. Line C illustrates the conversation that the director and the directee are having. In this conversation, the director is primarily helping the directee to say more about his interior affective movements and is checking to see if the directee has related these movements to God. Since line C — the conversation between director and directee — is the most evident and visibly obvious, it can unfortunately become the main focus. The director can unconsciously slip into the role of teacher or problem solver rather than a contemplative spiritual director.

In this contemplative approach to spiritual direction, the director helps the directee to not only understand his relationship with God better, but to fully enter into this relationship and to engage in it. "Spiritual direction of this kind focuses on what happens when a person listens to and responds to a self-communicating God."[*] This listening and responding is the content of line A in the above diagram.

Since the conversation between God and the directee is the focal point of contemplative spiritual direction, it is important that the directee bring to spiritual direction the content of his conversation with God. Just as food ingredients are essential to cooking, so is religious experience essential to spiritual direction. If one has no ingredients, a meal cannot be made. In the same way, if a directee has no experiences of God to speak about, there can be no spiritual direction in the proper sense.[†] Without religious experience to speak of, the spiritual direction conversation degenerates into a sharing on other topics: how ministry

---

[*]Barry and Connolly, *The Practice of Spiritual Direction*, 7.
[†]Ibid., 8.

is going, how family life is going, or even how the person thinks his spiritual life is going in a general sense. While each one of these areas is important and could possibly be part of the spiritual direction conversation, these topics do not get at the heart of the matter. Contemplative spiritual direction, in other words, "is directly concerned with a person's actual experiences of the relationship with God."‡

Given the importance of the directee's lived experience of his personal relationship with the Lord as being the subject of the spiritual direction conversation, the question could be raised: What happens if the directee consistently does not bring such contemplative experience to the spiritual direction conversation? If such is the case, it will be important for the spiritual director to try to discern what is happening in the directee's heart. It could be that the directee is having a contemplative spiritual experience but does not know how to name his inner experiences and needs to be accompanied in order to become more attentive to and to be able to name what the Lord is already doing in his life. On the other hand, it could be that the directee is struggling to place his relationship with God at the very center of his life — he lacks the necessary thirst for personal and intimate communion with Jesus Christ.

The deacon who seems to lack a desire for intimacy with God may be in need of a closer encounter with the Lord so that he might have an awakened heart. If such efforts at fostering intimacy seem to be unsuccessful, i.e., the deacon does not seem to have the openness of heart to experience more of the Lord, it may be that this deacon is not a good candidate for contemplative spiritual direction. Perhaps a recommendation can be made that he take some time away for a personal retreat so that his relationship with the Lord can be renewed. In the case of a man in formation for the permanent diaconate who seems to lack open-

---

‡Ibid.

ness to encountering the Lord personally, this resistance to God should cause him to reconsider whether or not he is truly being called to holy orders.

The Distinctiveness of Diaconal Spirituality

For anyone undertaking the spiritual direction of a permanent deacon, it is critical for the director to have at least a basic understanding of the diaconate and the manner in which the deacon's vocation plays an essential role in his interior life.

Understood correctly, the deacon's vocation is not a static call that, once fulfilled at ordination, is complete. In fact, because of his configuration to Christ the Servant, the call of God continues to resound in his heart in deeper and more profound ways. This is because the call is not so much something, the diaconate, but through the diaconate to some One, intimate communion with Christ the Servant. This is precisely why the spiritual director should be well versed in the spirituality of the diaconate.

When the term "diaconal spirituality" is used in popular literature, its meaning is often assumed. The context of its usage implies the way a deacon draws close to Christ through such practices as *lectio divina*, various devotions, spiritual direction, frequent confession, and Eucharistic adoration. While all of these have great merit in cultivating the interior life, in themselves they do not constitute a diaconal spirituality as such, but instead elements in the spirituality of a deacon. This may seem like a distinction without a difference, but, upon closer examination, the difference is vast.

To be sure, a deacon may and should participate in these devotions, but it's not only that he participates, but rather how this participation reflects his configuration to Christ the Servant. All of these devotions are a way of relating to God, and that relationship changed radically on the day of his ordination. Because he "is" deacon, because he has been indelibly marked as Christ the Servant, he now has the capacity of relating to God in a particular way, in a diaconal way. Since this relationship is contextualized as a gift of divine love outpoured, and since love cannot remain static, the essential characteristic and distinctive feature of diaconal spirituality is to grow in more intimate communion with Christ the Servant. In many respects, this not only defines diaconal spirituality, but the deacon himself, and becomes the source and strength of his ministry. It imbues his ministry with a particular quality, the quality of a servant who loves his Master tenderly.

The above definition uses the term "diaconal spirituality" in a collective sense. What is really meant is "diaconal spiritualities." There's not any one way to grow in greater communion with Christ the Servant, but many. As we have already seen, intimate communion implies a relationship, and a relationship always implies the union of two or more individuals. While Christ the Servant is a constant in the relationship, deacons are not. They represent a widely diverse group and, while there are many commonalities among them, the manner in which they encounter Christ, and allow him to accompany them on their vocational journey, will differ.

Just as no one person can image God, so no one person can incarnate Christ the Servant. The diversity of diaconal spiritualities reflects the diversity of men called to sacred service in the diaconate, and only together do they reveal Christ the Servant. In this way, they enable the ministry to permeate and penetrate all aspects of society.

Thus the uniqueness of diaconal spirituality — what sets it apart from other spiritualities — lies in the deacon's mystical identification with Christ the Servant. While all are called to serve by virtue of their baptism, the deacon is called to be an icon of Christ the Servant and, in this respect, he acts in the person of that same Christ who came not to be served, but to serve. This grounds diaconal spirituality in a specific kind of vocational relationship to God. It's a relationship that begins as an unfulfilled calling, beckoning him to a life lived in sacred ecclesial service. It's realized when his bishop says the prayer of ordination and lays hands upon him. It continues throughout his life as he exercises his diaconal ministry. Because he is deacon by virtue of his ordination, every act that proceeds from him has the capacity to be diaconal.

The Interplay Between Spiritual Direction & Pastoral Counseling

In the course of spiritual direction, the directee might bring up issues that could possibly be better discussed with a pastoral counselor or psychologist. It is important for the director to know the signs indicating that it would be best to refer the directee to a counselor/psychologist. However, even if such a referral is made, the spiritual director could still help the directee to "relate" these issues to the Lord in prayer. In this way, spiritual direction and counseling can complement each other. For example, a counselor might help a person to better articulate what he is experiencing emotionally, and once the person has this greater self-awareness, the spiritual director can help the person to speak to God about his experience. This conversation with God enables the directee to receive more Divine Love in the depths of his heart, which can lead to significant healing on many levels of the person's being.

SIMILARITIES of
Spiritual Direction and Counseling[§]

Both talk about the life experience of a person.

Neither uses an authoritarian approach.

Both facilitate individuals' growth in freedom.

Both favor development and process rather than abrupt change or precipitated change.

Both require trust.

Both require careful listening, empathy, care, and interest on part of counselor and director.

Resistance, transference, countertransference, and defense mechanisms occur in both.

Insight and healing occur through both.

Both look to change an attitude, better outlook on life, inner peace, and resolution of a conflict.

Both extend over a period of time.

DIFFERENCES	Spiritual Direc-tion	Coun-seling
Insight and healing occur primarily through the relationship and dialogue between God and directee, and secondarily through the relationship between director and directee.	Yes	No
Insight and healing takes place through relationship and dialogue between counselor and client.	No	Yes
There is a contemplative atmosphere, a conscious and affective awareness of God's presence; savoring, reliving, entering into experiences of God.	Yes	No
An awareness of God's presence need not be there at all. God's presence may be in the background, but not brought into the session in a conscious way.	No	Yes
The spiritual director spends time noticing, savoring, reliving, helping a person share feelings with God and be attentive to God's presence; sharing from feelings and not only about feelings.	Yes	No
The counselor, in their approach or process, spends time more in reflection, talking about feelings and issues, and making connections.	No	Yes

The Permanent Deacon as Spiritual Directee

The permanent deacon, as a spiritual directee, is somewhat unique from the perspective of his ordination and simultaneous connection with the secular world. He is a member of the clergy, but he typically has a wife and family. He has a job (unless he is retired) and a mortgage and the same day-to-day responsibilities of the lay faithful, but he is not a layman. He is called to a life of service, to the pursuit of holiness, to be an example or icon of Christ the Servant. Like all other clerics, he is the public face of the Church, even at work or while shopping with the wife and kids. He is a cleric, a member of the hierarchy of the Church who lives a primarily secular life. Having some understanding of these tensions should aid the director in providing spiritual direction to the deacon. The appendices contain information to further the spiritual director's understanding of the permanent diaconate.

The director should consider that the deacon is called to integrate the responsibilities and dynamics of family life, secular employment, ministry needs, recreation, and parish relationships. To do this well a deacon must have a deep spiritual life that permeates and informs these varied, and sometimes competing, facets of his life.

This understanding of the deacon will certainly be of utmost importance in the spiritual director's conversation with the deacon as a directee. A review of the deacon's prayer life is essential in helping him see the direction his life is taking. Is he regularly availing himself of the Sacrament of Penance (Reconciliation)? Is he faithful to the mandate to pray at least Morning and Evening Prayer from the Liturgy of the Hours? Is he reading Scripture regularly? Is he reading other good spiritual books? Is he keeping Christ at the center? Is he in relationship with Mary? Is his spiritual life a priority, or is it getting lost in the multitude of other responsibilities?

The married deacon should recognize the importance of his

responsibility to his sacramental union with his wife. In doing so, he needs to be open to the needs of his family, consisting of wife, children, and possibly grandchildren. Time spent with his family is important to maintaining a healthy family life. One of the most valuable services a deacon can offer the Church is a healthy, stable family.

It is extremely easy for a deacon to become too involved in his ministry and to accept the many invitations by parishioners to lead various meetings or prayer activities. Saying "no" is not easy for a deacon, especially when he knows that there is a need to be of service in his community. The deacon should maintain an open and honest conversation with his wife about his time commitments. She can be a valuable governor to prevent him from overcommitting himself. This relationship should never be compromised or neglected for the sake of ministry and should be fostered in a loving, prayerful home. From time to time the deacon may need the assistance of his spiritual director to remind him of this priority.

Parish life presents its own unique set of challenges. Is the deacon having any communication difficulties in his relationships with his pastor, other priests in the parish, and/or the parish staff? Spiritual guidance here is most valuable to help him assess the impact of his parish activities and relationships on his overall life balance.

Another area to consider for discussion might be focused on the deacon's secular work schedule. Does he travel for work, and if so, how often? Does he work weekends and/or long hours? His job, of course, is important to the welfare of his family, but it must be considered in the overall integration of his life and the impact it has on him and his family.

Harmony of life is very important for everyone and especially in the diverse life aspects of the deacon. Attempting to integrate ministry, secular work, spouse and family, liturgical and personal prayer, rest and recreation along with continuing study makes for a challenging and often stress-filled life. The spiritual director's assistance to the deacon, under the guidance of the Holy Spirit, in frequently assessing his activities and priorities will greatly aid the deacon as he attempts to integrate his busy life and give glory to God.

All relationships, whether family, work, or ministry, flow from and are directed back to the covenant relationship with God through His Church. Integrating all these various relationships is critical to maintaining the health of those relationships. Spiritual direction can be very helpful in assisting the deacon to do this successfully.

It is possible to harmonize the obligations of family life, work, and ministry. The key for any Christian is to keep Christ at the center of all the obligations of life. This is even more critical for an ordained cleric. The interior life of the spirit must be encouraged through regular spiritual direction.

The graphic below may help to illustrate how important it is for the deacon to keep his intimate, personal relationship with Christ at the center of his life. When Christ is at the center, Christ will inform and affect all the other aspects of the deacon's life.

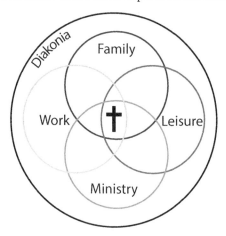

It may be helpful for a priest who is serving as the spiritual director for a deacon to review these thoughts from Deacon James Keating:

> For such a "simple" station in the church's hierarchy, the vocation of the deacon is complex. The complexity arises from the net of relationships in which the deacon finds himself upon ordination, a net that is not to be escaped but embraced. Unfortunately, the intricacy of the relationships of the diaconate can tempt a man to despair as he makes efforts to please all of his constituencies: wife, children, bishop, pastor, employer, parishioners, diocesan officials, fellow deacons, and more. Along with these relationships and the various calls they carry, the deacon also feels pressed to "perform" well in his ministries, which can be various and often emotionally consuming. However, looking at the vocation of deacon from the perspective of what Christ is sharing with him, the deacon can receive clarity on a vital truth: it is not the quantity of acts of service that matter to Christ, but simply one's fidelity to the character of ordination. Excessive activity and neurotic hand-wringing about whether "I am *doing enough* to help others" gives birth only to stress, not to holiness.[5]

For a deacon to remain healthy and effective, he must give priority to his spiritual life. As a man devoted to service, it can be a temptation to focus on the externals of "doing" rather than on being. A deacon is called to a simple lifestyle, to pray with and for the Church in the Liturgy of the Hours, to frequent reception of the sacraments, to personal piety, and to a deep interior relationship with Christ, Mother Mary, and the saints. All Christians

---

[5] *The Heart of the Diaconate*, 49.

are called to holiness. For clerics, both priests and deacons, the public nature of their sacramental identity adds another layer to that call. Good spiritual direction will encourage the deacon to deepen his interior life, foster intimacy with the Lord, and learn to discern the movements of the Spirit in his heart.

Practical Considerations

On a practical level, the following elements will help guide the spiritual direction process:

- **Frequency and length of spiritual direction sessions:** It is recommended that a deacon receive spiritual direction about once per month, or every six weeks at the most. Spiritual direction sessions would normally be about one hour in length.
- **Scheduling appointments:** In order to ensure that spiritual direction is a real priority for the deacon, the deacon and his director should be intentional about scheduling appointments ahead of time. One way to do this would be to schedule the next appointment at the end of each session. Alternatively, the deacon and his director could schedule out several appointments six months at a time.
- **Location of spiritual direction sessions:** In order to preserve the serious and confidential nature of the spiritual direction relationship, sessions should take place in a private setting such as the priest's office or other suitable place, rather than in a more public and social environment such as a restaurant or café.
- **Personal prayer:** In addition to praying the Liturgy of the Hours every day, as promised at ordination, it is strongly recommended that the deacon spend at least half an hour of personal prayer each day with the

Sacred Scriptures. There are various expressions of personal prayer as referenced in the *Catechism of the Catholic Church*: vocal prayer, meditation, and contemplative prayer (2700–2719). The deacon's prayer might gravitate toward any of these forms, but what is most important is that his prayer be focused on growing in his intimate, personal relationship with the Lord. This time of personal prayer is the basis for the conversation that the deacon will have with his spiritual director. If the deacon is not taking this time for daily personal prayer, there will not be much for him to talk about in spiritual direction.

• **Journaling:** It is recommended that the deacon keep a personal prayer journal. In this journal the deacon can regularly record key aspects of his ongoing conversation with the Lord. Some key data to include would be: the Scripture passage that was prayed with, the graces the deacon was asking for, the key movements of the deacon's heart (i.e., thoughts, feelings, desires), what the Lord did or not did seem to be doing in the deacon's heart, etc. The deacon can then review his journal entries from the past month and let this review be the basis for his conversation with his spiritual director.

• **Sacrament of Penance:** it is recommended that a deacon receive the Sacrament of Penance on a regular basis. The Church clearly calls us to "hold in high esteem the frequent use of this sacrament. It is a practice which increases true knowledge of one's self, favors Christian humility and offers the occasion for salutary spiritual direction and the increase of grace."** Specifically, the recommendation to religious states

---

** Sacred Congregation for Religious and the Secular Institutes, *Decree on Confession for Religious*, par. 3.

the following: "desiring closer union with God, [we] should endeavor to receive the sacrament of penance frequently, that is, twice a month."[††] Indeed, this is advice that all ordained clergy would do well to follow.

The First Meeting

A suggested approach to the first spiritual direction meeting might follow this plan:[‡‡]

1. Determine: "What does a person want?"
   a. Clarify the expectations of the deacon.
   b. Notice signs of religious experience.
   c. Verify the desire to grow in prayer and the desire to grow in relationship with the Lord.

2. Move toward establishing a "contract"
   d. State your understanding of spiritual direction.
   e. Name the specifics of time, place, duration, evaluation, and supervision.
   f. Determine whether or not the person agrees.

3. Remainder of the session: two approaches
   g. Share biography and history of their relationship with the Lord.
   -or-
   h. Share how the Lord is being experienced now.

[††]Ibid.
[‡‡]Adapted from a text by Maureen Conroy, RSM, from the Upper Room Spiritual Center in Neptune, New Jersey.

ACKNOWLEDGMENTS

In the pursuit of knowledge, be it theological or pastoral, the journey is never solitary. It's marked by the wisdom, guidance, and support of remarkable individuals who illuminate the path and inspire the pursuit of truth. With profound gratitude, I acknowledge those whose contributions have graced these pages and enriched the tapestry of this work.

Most Reverend Ronald A. Hicks
Diocese of Joliet
Your unwavering commitment to the Faith and solid leadership have illuminated the way, leading me toward a deeper understanding of clerical unity. Your presence in these pages is a testament to your dedication to the Church and her mission.

Most Reverend David J. Bonnar
Diocese of Youngstown
Your theological wisdom and your tireless dedication to fostering the growth of faith have left an indelible mark on this work. Your insights and guidance, particularly from the perspective of bishops and priests, are sincerely appreciated.

Msgr. Denis DuPont-Fauville
Former Director of the Diaconate, Archdiocese of Paris
From across the sea, your wisdom and theological acumen have bridged the gap and enriched the discourse within these pages. Your global perspective and profound insights concerning the nature of the Church have contributed immeasurably to the depth and breadth of this work.

Rev. Gregory Rothfuchs
Pastor of St. Joseph Church in Lockport, Diocese of Joliet
Your theological expertise, your experience as a pastor working with deacons, and your passion for truth have been a guiding light throughout the creation of this book. Your commitment to your own priesthood as my pastor and my friend has affirmed the value of clerical unity and the fruit it bears.

Deacon James Keating
Professor of Spiritual Theology, Kenrick-Glennon Seminary, Archdiocese of St. Louis
Your profound understanding of the diaconate and its spiritual significance has greatly enriched our exploration of this vocation. Your insights into the interior life have brought depth and authenticity to these pages, as they have in my own life and ministry.

Deacon Victor Puscas
Director of Diaconal Formation, Diocese of Joliet
Your dedication to the diaconate and your unwavering commitment to the Church's mission have left an indelible mark on me and, through me, this work. Your perspectives and experiences have lent practical authenticity to this discussion.

To each of you and many others, I offer our deepest appreciation and heartfelt gratitude for your invaluable contributions. Your wisdom, guidance, and unwavering support have been instrumental in the writing of this book. May your continued journey be filled with blessings and grace.

ABOUT THE AUTHOR

Deacon Dominic Cerrato is the director of diaconal formation for the Diocese of Joliet, Illinois. He also serves as executive director of Diaconal Ministries, a national ministry developed under Bishop Jeffrey Monforton of the Archdiocese of Detroit that ministers to permanent deacons and those they serve. Deacon Dominic was ordained a Roman Catholic permanent deacon in 1995 for the Diocese of Steubenville, Ohio. He earned a PhD in theology from the Catholic Theological Foundation via Duquesne University in 2009, a master's in theology from Duquesne University, and a bachelor's in theology from Franciscan University in Steubenville, Ohio.

Deacon Dominic is editor of *The Deacon* magazine and author of several books, including *Encountering Christ the Servant: A Spirituality of the Diaconate* (OSV, 2020). He is a member of both the Fellowship of Catholic Scholars and the National Association of Diaconate Directors, and he serves as director of spiritual direction for the Pastoral Solutions Institute in Steubenville. He has been married to Judith Cerrato since 1982, and the couple has seven children and many grandchildren.

You might also like:

Encountering Christ the Servant: A Spirituality of the Diaconate
By Deacon Dominic Cerrato, PhD

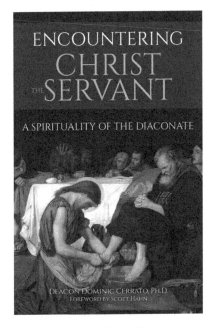

This book offers deacons and deacon candidates an integrated approach to diaconal life and ministry, rooted in the cultivation of the interior life. In this study, Deacon Dominic outlines the primacy of the interior life, the necessity of abandonment, the sacrament of the present moment, and living the Servant Mysteries.

Entering into a new and more intimate relationship with Christ the Servant will open deacons and deacon candidates to their true identity, and their mission, as heralds of the Gospel of Christ.

You might also like:

Ars Celebrandi:
Serving the Mystery of Christ in the Eucharist
By Reverend Gerald Dennis Gill

Every aspect of the Eucharist matters. The Church provides clear guidance for the celebration of the sacred mysteries for the benefit of the ordained and the baptized to encounter these saving mysteries.

This book walks through each part of the Mass, discussing the directives for the celebration through the lens of the *ars celebrandi*, to help priests, deacons, and seminarians authentically join with Christ in his eternal Sacrifice with deeper faith, confidence, and reverence.

Available at
OSVCatholicBookstore.com
or wherever books are sold

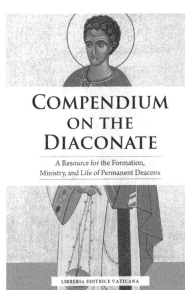

Discovering Christ the Servant: A Spirituality of Service

By Deacon Dominic Cerrato, PhD

Because Jesus came not to be served but to serve (Mk 10:45), his Mystical Body, the Church, is essentially a servant Church. It's precisely through this service that she carries out her mission.

The ancient diaconate was instituted, and has been restored in our time, not simply to stand alongside priestly, religious, and lay ministry but to imbue and empower each with a renewed sense of service. Indeed, the Greek word *diakonia*, which is translated in English as "service," can also be translated into the Latin word *ministerium*, translated in English as "ministry." Thus, when we look at episcopal ministry, priestly ministry, religious ministry, or lay ministry, service is essential to all.

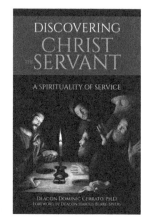

"In *Discovering Christ the Servant*, Deacon Cerrato has provided a concise yet detailed spiritual roadmap leading to a deeper understanding of lay service. What surprised me was his approach: developing a lay spirituality of service by looking through the lens of diaconal service. Absolutely brilliant!" — From the foreword by Deacon Harold Burke-Sivers

You might also like:

How to Make Homilies Better, Briefer, and Bolder
By Alfred McBride, O.Praem.

Sincere, encouraging, and downright practical, Father McBride's *How to Make Homilies Better, Briefer, and Bolder* makes it easy to connect with your parishioners every Sunday and help them apply their faith to real life. Blending simple-to-follow instructions, proven strategies, and the occasional rule, this guidebook encapsulates 50 years of sermon mastery from one of the most notable preachers of our time.

How to Make Homilies Better, Briefer, *and* Bolder

Tips from a Master Homilist

Alfred McBride, O.Praem.

Preface by Archbishop Timothy M. Dolan

Comprehensive yet compact, this book includes practical steps for overcoming public-speaking fears and time-saving tips for finding relevant stories that warrant sharing.

Available at
OSVCatholicBookstore.com
or wherever books are sold